Passport to Freedom

"Just a fan letter to congratulate you on the draft of your forthcoming books, of which I read a good part. It is a handbook of outstanding example, not one of how to create revolutions, how to blow up temples, how to destroy human beings, of which there are many current, but one of how to make human beings into solid, inspiring, courageous men and women of integrity. I applaud and congratulate you on the destination of your life's work."

—Sir Yehudi Menuhin

"Garry Davis's new book is an inspiring contribution to securing individual human rights and freedoms and to creating a new and far-reaching consciousness for mankind. [He] has made a great contribution to raising humanity's consciousness towards planetary unity. He is World Citizen Number One."

—Michio Kushi
Founder, Macrobiotic World Movement

I am eager to express to the . . . war veteran Davis my recognition of the sacrifice he has made for the well-being of humanity. In voluntarily giving up his citizenship rights he has made of himself a 'displaced person' in order to fight for the natural rights of those who are the mute evidences of the low moral levels of our time."

—Albert Einstein
Telegram to Salle Pleyel Meeting, 1948

"Garry Davis is right. War and nationalism often go together. 'National Security' is the real scourge of our time. Passport to Freedom guides us in a better way to seize the new opportunities opened up by the end of the Cold War."

—Rear Adm. Gene R. LaRocque
U.S. Navy Retired, Director,
Center for Defense Information

"I share the basic impulses that motivate your activity. It is ahead of its time, but embodies an outlook that needs to become accepted if our species is to endure and survive."

—Richard Falk
Center of International Studies, Princeton University

"The pioneering work you have done, your commitment to world peace through world authority and globsl citizenship are genuine contributions to both of these causes."

—Saul Mendlowitz
World Policy Institute

Passport to Freedom

A Guide for World Citizens

Garry Davis

with Greg Guma

Seven Locks Press
Washington

Library of Congress Cataloging-in-Publication Data

Passport to Freedom: a guide for world citizens /
Garry Davis with Greg Guma
    p.   cm.
ISBN 0-929765-08-7 (cloth): $24.95
ISBN 0-929765-07-9 (paper): $12.95
1. Internationalism. I. Guma, Greg. II. Title
JC361.D359   1991
327.1'7—dc20   91-35805
                                              CIP

For more information contact:

Seven Locks Press
P.O. Box 27
Cabin John, MD 20818

To the 600 million plus stateless, embryos-to-be-humans, unclassified, ethnically indifferent, legally undefined and cosmically pacific, about to freely immigrate from Beyond in innocent and unadorned wonder onto spaceship Earth, a minor space-time world of fellow humans and fellow species. May they enlighten we who have forgotten our Source.

CONTENTS

Introduction   ix

Prologue: A Lover's Lesson   1

Part One: Reclaiming Your Sovereignty

Divided World   7
One World or None   9
Humanity's Mandate: The Universal Declaration
     of Human Rights   11
Identity Lost   14
Paper Power   16
The Sources of Sovereignty   18
Identity Found   22
Four Levels of Identity   24
Bureaucratic Territory   26
Learning the Language   28
How to Overrule Bureaucracies: Ten Steps   30
A World Citizen Comes Home   42
Transcending Nationalism   45

Part Two: Crossing Frontiers

State of the Nation-State   53
Allegiance to Insecurity   56
The Passport Swindle   59
     Unsafe Passage   61
     Perpetual Harassment   63
     Above & Beyond   65
The World Passport: Tool & Symbol   66
Credo of a World Citizen   70
World Citizenship — The Basics   71
Proof of Rights   77
     World Marriage Certificate   77
     World Political Asylum Card   78
     International Exit Visa   79
     International Resident Permit   79

Using Your Passport   81
    Gaining Acceptance   81
    Transcending Rejection   84
Travel Log: 1977–1984   89

Part Three: The Global Contract

Searching for Higher Authority   119
What is World Government?   125
    How It Began   126
    How It Works   127
The Non-Military Alternative   130
    World Birth Certificate   131
    World Guards   132
    From Objection to Projection   133
    The Sleeping Giant   134
Territory: A Worldly View   136
    On Legal Ground   137
    International Homeland: 1948   139
    Mundialization   140
Economics: Toward Mutual Affluence   145
    Democratic Ownership   149
    World Money   150
    Economic Rights   152
The Practice of Freedom   156
    Planetary Process   157
    Points of Entry   159
Pledge of Allegiance   165
Epilog: A Borderless World Order   166

Appendices

World Government of World Citizens   175
List of Nation-States   176
Universal Declaration of Human Rights   179
Index   187

Introduction

The message of this book is as simple as it is revolutionary: the system of exclusive nation-states poses the greatest single threat to humanity, and the only alternative is to replace it with world law and a democratically-controlled world government. As the 20th Century careens to an end, the inability of nations to resolve major problems facing their citizens — in fact, their propensity to create problems, is further exposed with each passing day. At the same time, national leaders reveal their blind drive for power under a thin disguise; these so-called defenders of the public trust, these protectors of national security, betray humanity's trust and promote global insecurity. Facing these harsh realities, more and more people search desperately for a route to salvation. It is for all these explorers that *Passport to Freedom* has been written.

In virtually every corner of the world, millions of people already view themselves as world citizens. For these partners in the new "global contract," this guidebook is designed to increase their effectiveness and deepen their analysis. For those working in allied groups — from peace organizations to other One World formations, it is both a statement of solidarity and a challenge. The challenge is to move beyond reactive responses to crises and instead take a bold and pro-active approach to the creation of world peace. We will not have peace or justice until the scourge of nationalism is neutralized. This book provides both theoretical and practical means toward that goal. Beyond this "organized" world public, however, is a vast sea of concerned but not yet "worldly" citizens. They are fed up with their leaders and politics as usual. They know that, around the world, "the scoundrels are in power." They are mad as hell, but feel helpless to do anything about it. Effective solutions to either immediate or long-term problems have so far eluded their grasp. For them, this book is a reminder: the world is your country — but only if you claim it.

No doubt some readers will be skeptical, perhaps even pessimistic, and only swayed by unassailable arguments and demonstrable truths. Like Arjuna in the Bhagavad Gita, they may be closest to emancipation . . . and furthest from knowing it, just as the noon-day sun casts the deepest shadows. But a converted skeptic can sometimes become a sage. For the skeptics, then, this book provides numerous practical examples of the nation-state's impotence when confronted with the powerful logic of world citizenship.

Finally, for the youth, who express understandable confusion when faced with the bitter fruit of nationalism — barbaric wars, here is a call: the world is yours, so take it. This book is your tool. Your parents can do no more than build a bridge to One World. But you can cross it and reach the other side.

***

We have called it a guide, and it is. But this book also presents the theoretical framework for the world citizenship movement, as well as some moments in its four decade history. And because it is meant to both inspire and entertain, you will find a variety of vignettes that illustrate the basic points of the text.

In Part One, both the nature of sovereignty and the problem of bureaucracy are explored. In order to neutralize bureaucrats, you must know your rights. Therefore, the *Universal Declaration of Human Rights* is described in some detail. A practical, step-by-step approach to handling bureaucrats is also provided. This approach, stressing knowledge, proof and confidence, is based on decades of personal experience and the cases of many refugees for whom human rights are the only protection against nation-state tyranny.

After describing the development and inevitable demise of the nation-state global system, Part Two outlines its use of passports to turn citizens into global subjects, and then presents a powerful alternative: the World Passport. In a clear question-and-answer format, the basics of world citizenship are defined. Procedures for using the World Passport and other World Service Authority documents, including the World Marriage Certificate, World Political Asylum Card, International Exit Visa, and International Resident Permit, are also included.

The log of my travels between 1977 and 1984, at the end of Part Two, opens questions concerning the arbitrary nature of U.S.

immigration law, the collusion of airlines and governments in denying travel rights, and the extremes to which some governments will go in order to avoid dealing with the profound implications of World Government. Since it is also the story of an unusual journey, however, you may find much of it entertaining, even funny.

For those ready to take the leap and become citizens of the world, Part Three offers a new home: the World Government of World Citizens, which has been operating since 1953. In this part, you will read about World Government's early history, as well as its implications in areas such as military service, territory and economics. In particular, the development of the Sovereign Order of World Guards is a ready-made alternative to national military service, supported by international law and the U.S. Constitution, for conscientious objectors and others who would rather work for peace than kill for "national security." Concepts such as World Territory, the related "mundialization" movement, a global economic system based on Mutual Affluence, and World Money are also described. In a final chapter, the process for development of a World Constitution, using revolutionary cybernetic techniques, is explained. Suggestions for anyone ready to declare him or herself a World Citizen are also offered.

In the life of any movement, there comes a critical point when external events and the internal evolution of the movement itself converge to create conditions for radical change. It does not always happen, of course. Opportunities are often missed, and many movements dissipate. For World Citizenship, this turning point has arrived. With the nation-state system facing stress on all fronts, who can any longer deny that a new World Order is absolutely vital. The question is: what kind of order? A tyrannical, top-down dictatorship which denies individual sovereignty? A Total State controlled by the few shareholders in Multinationals? An impotent federation, dominated by the most powerful industrial nations?

Or a World Government, democratically controlled by all its citizens, which recognizes their individual sovereignty as well as the ultimate sovereignty of humanity as a whole? In the hope that the last option can and will be taken, this guidebook is offered for those ready to save and transform the world. You need not take all its arguments on faith. You are welcome — in fact, challenged

— to put them to practical tests. If you do, I am confident that you will find that World Citizenship is truly your passport to freedom.

Garry Davis
November 1, 1991

Prologue

A Lover's Lesson

Rays of sunlight filtered through the foliage in the forest at Ootacamond in the Nilgiris in South India. After the hurly-burly of America and Europe in the mid-1950s, the mild climate, immense calm and homely yet strangely impersonal kindness of my host were soothing. Strolling under the stately trees, Nataraja Guru turned to me. "To be a lover of humanity," he said, "one must first acknowledge its existence. This is difficult for most people to do. It means giving up many false notions."

We continued our walk in silence.

A lover of humanity. I'd never heard the phrase before. How could one love all humanity? I wondered. Wasn't love a strictly personal emotion, what you might feel for some individual, your family, some sport, or perhaps a favorite food? If so, how could you identify personally with all humanity? It's hard enough to even grasp the concept of humanity, let alone "love" it.

Looking deeper, I recalled my avid reading of science fiction as a teenager. In many a tale "humanity" faced some alien race from a distant galaxy. The "home" planet was usually Mother Earth, and I had come to regard this as only natural. Thanks to writers like Isaac Asimov, Arthur Clarke Jr. and Ted Sturgeon, I had been able to "leave home" mentally, and then return with a new appreciation.

Still, accepting the existence of something called humanity — and loving it, as the guru advised — required an enormous leap in comprehension. It meant moving far beyond the love of family, friends or even nation. Certainly, the notion was logical. Each of these smaller groups derived from common humanity, I thought. Perhaps it was mere ignorance to love the part without acknowledging the whole. As I pondered, the Guru stopped and looked at me, his head slightly cocked.

1

"I think you are a true lover of humanity," he said.

As I stared at him, my feelings were mixed. Love and humanity were not yet linked in my mind. One was personal, the other abstract. Yet I was pleased — though I didn't fully know why. Perhaps I somehow sensed the truth and even the necessity of the relationship he had described.

***

In the years since that Spring day in 1956 I have gradually come to understand what he meant. I've also discovered more about the choices and commitments a lover of humanity must make.

These days many people are willing to acknowledge the existence of humanity and proclaim its right to survive. But that is still not the same as "loving" it. The person in love is ready and willing to die for it. And of course, millions of people are willing to die for their country, or their faith, when it is threatened. But for humanity? For planet Earth?

Since World War II, however, the threats to humanity have become increasingly apparent. Still more shocking, we have learned that the enemy is truly ourselves. In the attempt to dominate nature and other human beings, we have left a trail of misery, poverty and devastation. In less than a century we have disrupted the ecology of the entire planet, a change that dwarfs almost every previous event in human history. Through ignorance of the essential unity of humanity, our species has jeopardized its own existence.

In the 1940s, Nataraja Guru already could see the solution. While teaching at the International School in Geneva, he would listen to the daily broadcasts of United Nations debates and think about what was missing. The UN had only recently been formed, but the Guru quickly pinpointed the flaw. No one represented humanity. Among all the delegates from nation-states, no one was willing to put the interest of the whole above the needs or policies of particular nations. In that sense at least, not much has changed since 1945.

When I met him in 1950, after renouncing my national citizenship, he said that my act of conscience was the equivalent of an Indian taking a vow of Sannyasin, a requirement for wisdom-seeking. The idea that I was looking for wisdom instead of a political solution to the war-making of nations seemed ludicrous at first.

Six years later I went to India as his student, and returned as a "lover of humanity." Since then I've learned the fulfilling lesson that the maturing of wisdom develops along with the capacity to love. In fact, love is the cup that wisdom fills.

Today, however, the injunction to "love humanity" is no longer just some altruistic sentiment. For the health of the planet and the survival of humanity, as well as other species, it has become a categorical imperative.

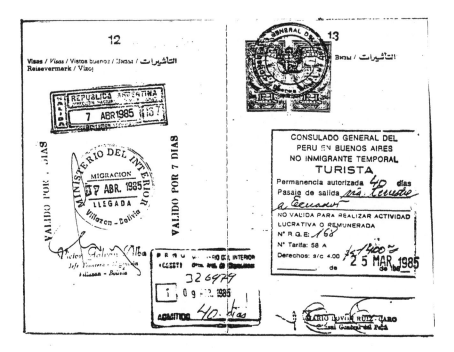

This visa and other visas reproduced in this book come from pages of World Service Authority passports.

Reclaiming Your Sovereignty

Chapter 1

Divided World

We are born as citizens of the world. But we are also born into a divided world, a world of separate entities called nations. We may regard each other as friends, and yet we are separated by wide, artificially created barriers. Whatever we may think of one another, each one of us on this planet is designated as "alien" by billions of his or her fellow humans. The label applies to everyone who does not share our status as a "national citizen." And many millions of us, despite our religious, ethnic or racial kinship, are forced to wear another label: enemy.

I first became aware of all this during the second world war, while flying over Germany as a bomber pilot. In that starkly realistic situation, behind all the emotion and hysteria, I was forced to consider for the first time the foolishness of one group of human beings dropping bombs on another group.

There were, obviously, good reasons for my participation in the fight. Fascism was a public menace, a social disease that had to be wiped out. But even so, I had to wonder what was wrong with the organization of the human community when a social disease like fascism was allowed to become such a plague that only an opposing plague could halt its advance. I wasn't alone. Millions of young people were being rudely shocked into the awareness that the social plague called war was a part of their lives.

After the war, even though we gained a supposedly supranational organization called the United Nations, the wondering — and the problems — continued. There was a brief flurry of post-war disarmament, and then the still absolutely sovereign states continued their superarmament race. The bombs went from "conventional" to "nuclear" — that is, from relative to absolute. A new word, "omnicide," was coined to define the awesome power now available to the world's politicians. Berlin became the focal point of the Cold War. Trouble brewed in Korea, Trieste, Israel, Jordan, Algeria, Kashmir, Malaya and Kenya. In the United States, taxes increased and funds for relief efforts were cut as defense budgets rose.

Eminent scientists warned that there was no defense against the absolute weapons being developed. Fear and insecurity became commonplace. In 1946, Albert Einstein concluded, "With all my heart I believe that the world's present system of sovereign nations can lead only to barbarism, war and inhumanity, and that only world law can assure progress towards a civilized peaceful community."

On our one and only planet, there were at the time about 80 separate and sovereign political and economic units. Today there are over 175. Some are rich, some poor. Some are large, others small. But all are the same in one respect: each claims absolute political power over its citizens. Like a body with 175 separate brains, each gives different orders to the various organs. If the Earth was a single human, we'd call him an uncoordinated idiot. As it is, the absence of a "world brain" is a state of being one can quite reasonably label global idiocy. And the United Nations? Wasn't it created in order to be the brain of humanity — an inclusive coordinating authority? Despite the noble convictions and imposing facade, the answer is a clear no. One of the clearest pieces of evidence is its complete failure to prevent war. Out of the 200 wars fought thus far in the 20th Century, at least 75 occurred after the founding of the UN.

The United Nations is at best a meeting place where representatives of most nation-states attempt to win world public opinion for their particular interests. Often it is even less, a smokescreen behind which the most powerful nations attempt to impose their nationalistic policies. The UN, sadly, is neither united nor inclusive.

Chapter 2

One World or None

As 1948 began I took a hard look at myself and the world around me. Neither sight was reassuring. Our ignorance was appalling, and we could find no reasonable answers to the vital questions of the day. The best brains on the planet said that World War III would put the world itself on the front line, and all we could do, apparently, was babble. Despite my confusion and the din of small talk, one phrase seemed to echo inside my head: "One world or none." Wendell Wilkie, the Republican Presidential candidate in 1940, had expressed it in his best-selling book, *One World*. The sentiment was repeated by Bertrand Russell, Albert Schweitzer, Gandhi and Einstein, eventually forcing me to recognize the provincialism of my own thinking.

In *Peace or Anarchy*, Cord Meyer proposed a world federation as the alternative to warring nations. Of course, I thought! This was the cure for the plague of war. Just as the individual states had joined together to form the federal United States, all nations could join a world federation. I began working with the United World Federalists, attending meetings and hammering out policies.

But something was missing, and world tensions were mounting too rapidly. I wanted a crusade, not meetings. The crisis was total. The commitment had to be total.

In addition, my studies had led me to the conclusion that war could not be permanently avoided through a partial sacrifice of sovereignty by the nations of the world. The roots of war were inherent in the nation-state itself, which exists separate and distinct. Radical as it may sound, to eliminate war, you would have to eliminate nations. But no nation was voluntarily going to dissolve itself.

A federation of nations thus appeared unworkable. If anything could be "federated" or united, it was people. The founders of the United States hadn't merely created a central government

9

for the various states. They had declared themselves Americans first, then Virginians, New Yorkers, and so on. To bring about world government, that step would again have to be taken. People would have to declare themselves citizens of the world and begin behaving as such.

But how could you practice world citizenship in a divided world? Could you be part of both humanity and a nation? Wouldn't your loyalties be divided? The answers eluded me until I read the story of Henry Noel, a young Harvard graduate who had renounced his U.S. citizenship and begun working as a laborer in Germany, rebuilding a bombed-out church. His was a bold, dramatic and logical protest against the illusory exclusive character of the state. It was also an affirmation of the fundamental sovereignty of the individual.

For me, this was the key to action and commitment. To become a citizen of the world, I decided, I would have to renounce my exclusive national allegiance.

Off with the old, and on with the new.

Chapter 3

Humanity's Mandate

On December 10, 1948, the *Universal Declaration of Human Rights* was adopted by the General Assembly of the United Nations. Forty-eight countries were in favor, including the United States, Great Britain, France, and India. None were opposed, but some members of the Communist bloc abstained.

The Declaration is the greatest mandate to organize ourselves rationally ever given to humanity as a corporate body. It contains the legal justifications for a variety of tactics that can be used by anyone attempting to assert his or her freedom to travel. It also embodies the basis for a revolutionary strategy to move us toward global unity. At the same time it implies that the United Nations as such is NOT the organization to create this unity. The mandate, says the Declaration, was given not to nations but instead to everyone on the planet. No one was excluded. Yet for more than four decades this milestone in our collective effort to achieve freedom and security has remained just another piece of paper with stirring words. Why? Because human rights apply only to humans. Until we declare ourselves as such—and organize along human lines so that practical leaders can represent us — we can only expect less than human treatment.

Let's consider what the Declaration provides for individuals and humanity as a whole.

The first article is a powerful tool that cuts through prejudice, dogma, artificial beliefs and general ignorance. All humans, it says, "are born free and equal in dignity and rights; they are endowed with reason and conscience and should act towards one another in a spirit of brotherhood." Right from the start, the *Declaration of Human Rights* affirms both a spiritual truth — that all of us are directly connected with our divine origin through individual conscience, and the endowment of reason — our ability to solve problems of survival and social relationship.

It also legitimizes the human species as such. As humans, we are born not into a political fiction called the "United States" or "Soviet Union." We are born into the entire world community, and into the family of humanity. These are dynamic facts. What they imply is that like the human right to live, legitimate and entitled to legal protection, the act of human birth is also legitimate.

Yet unlimited evidence demonstrates that, despite our fervent aspirations, utter foolishness rather than reason actually "governs" the world community. We, the people are inarticulate. Though we have reason and the guidance of conscience, we have no human representatives in politics. No one speaks for humanity as a whole.

Fortunately, the *Universal Declaration of Human Rights* goes further than merely proclaiming us free and equal. It mandates the right to organize a world electorate. "The will of the people," says Article 21 (3), "shall be the basis of the authority of government; this shall be expressed in periodic and genuine elections which shall be universal and equal suffrage and shall be held by secret vote or by equivalent free voting procedures."

THE people, it says. All the people. Not Americans, Russians, French, South Africans, or Japanese. Not Christians, Jews, Muslims, or Hindus. Not blacks, whites, yellows, or browns. The human community, it says, and not only the nations and people of the UN. This includes, of course, all stateless people and those under colonial domination. In short, this means that all of us, despite our differences, are part of this One People. Everybody's included — like it or not, accept it or not.

Article 21 also refers to a collective will. Does such a thing exist? you might well ask. Believe it or not, everyone does want just about the same things. But the slogans expressing them — peace, personal freedom, global well-being, universal harmony — have been distorted by hidden meanings. Over the centuries, people have become cynical and bitter. Nevertheless, the will to obtain these things still exists, and in greater quantity than most of us dream. In Article 28 of the Declaration, we receive a solid clue about the conditions under which our human rights can be secured. "Everyone," it states, "is entitled to the social and international order in which the rights and freedoms set forth in this declaration can be fully realized."

Order means, in essence, law and government. "International" is another way of describing the whole world. According to Article 28, then, we're entitled to world government as the way to claim our rights. From Manu's laws through the Decalogue, the Magna Carta, the Nuremberg Principles and the Universal Declaration, the human mind has been struggling to render order out of chaos. Every national constitution, however flawed, is a manifestation of our continued attempt to systematize the general good and make it consistent with the individual good. The one and the many, unity in diversity, all for one and one for all — all these dialectical formulas expressing the dual nature of human society.

We are also entitled to human rights, says Article 2, "without distinctions of any kind, such as race, color, sex, language, religion, political or other opinion, national or social origin, property, birth or other status." In short, we're all members of the same human community. There are no second class citizens of the world. Our human rights obviously unite us across all frontiers. And yet only a select few humans actually experience the freedoms promised in the Declaration. The truth is: no one can hand us freedom or security. And no one can exercise our reason and conscience on our behalf. Every one of us is absolutely and solely responsible for his or her thoughts and actions regarding our personal welfare. Only when we secure and use our conscience and reason will we discover the joyful world of sovereign humanity.

Chapter 4

Identity Lost

By the time the *Universal Declaration of Human Rights* was adopted, I had been a stateless person living in France for seven months. The French government wanted to expel me. The world press was intrigued — or at least highly amused.

What had I done? Simply put, I had seceded from the "exclusive" system of the nation-state. On the advice of the U.S. Attorney General, who had informed me that a citizen must be on foreign soil in order to legally renounce his or her nationality, I had chosen France. Once there I had presented myself at the U.S. Embassy.

"Think it over," said the Consul. "Come back Thursday." He wanted time to get instructions from Washington, he said.

When I returned six days later, he admitted that was a lie. "Just wanted to give you a little time to cool off."

I demanded the Oath of Renunciation, threatening to report him to Washington for neglect of duty. A few minutes later I was raising my right hand before the vice-consul while the Embassy secretaries gazed wide-eyed at this young, obviously crazy American, their typewriters silent.

Renouncing my citizenship was extremely frightening. I was cutting myself out of the entire nation-state system. From then on I would be "outside" looking "in." After I recited the Oath, the first thing the Vice-Consul did was ask for my U.S. passport — government property. At the time I hoped to demonstrate through this dramatic gesture that nations are a myth, perpetuated by the slavery of tradition, blind loyalty and pieces of paper that pretended to legitimize the existence of human beings. I would survive without papers, I thought. I would cross frontiers without a passport, acting as a free being without national credentials of any kind. I would strike a blow at the very heart of nationalism and prove that the nation-state didn't really exist but was only a creature of our minds.

The next day I went to the Prefecture de Police to explain my new and unique situation. A kind-looking women behind a large desk gave me an inquiring stare.

"I renounced my U.S. nationality yesterday," I said. "Now I am stateless. I don't want to break French laws. What should I do?" As I spoke, her eyes grew wide. After a pause, she bombarded me with questions: Why did I do it? Who was I really? How could she be sure I was Garry Davis? After all, anyone could walk in and say that. Where was the paper that proved my identity?

"I have no papers," I managed, "that's just the point. I think being a human being is more important than having papers. And since I'm here in France as a stranger, I'd like to know what I must do according to French law."

"According to French law," she replied despairingly, "you do not exist."

Chapter 5

Paper Power

Papers and documents, we are told, provide status, dignity and privileges. In a world divided into exclusive territories, they seem as necessary to survival as our lungs. Without them, after all, how can we breathe freely?

But do documents increase our sense of belonging in the human community, expand our awareness, or enhance our self-esteem? Obviously not. And more to the point, who or what gains most in the document game — the individual or the authority that issues them? After forty years outside the nation-state system, I see the sham for what it is. In fact, I'm living proof that conventional wisdom has it exactly backward. In each paper transaction, the individual is actually surrendering freedom. Instead, the documents legitimize the existence and privileges of the institution that provides the paper.

Whether it is a passport or driver's license, a degree or license to marry, the dynamic is the same. You surrender the right to assume command or determine your own direction by accepting some outside authority's power to grant these things. A person who hangs a degree on the office wall unwittingly admits that he has forfeited his power of discernment to an institution. The document says he is educated; education itself is thus vested in the institution. The degree is the graduate's receipt for having bargained away his intelligence. The person who provides the paper, usually a bureaucrat, doesn't think about such issues. Enmeshed in hierarchy, bureaucrats surrender their humanity and substitute anonymous power for individual personality. Ask for a bureaucrat's name and you'll often receive a brush-off. Personalizing the process is considered offensive, since the official is considered merely part of the machine.

The cog in the machine is anonymous, and acts without personal responsibility. The machine itself, meanwhile, has the power to dominate and punish anyone "inside" its domain. Documents are the central tools that consolidate and extend this power.

When I surrendered my passport in 1948, declaring myself a world citizen, with the intention of living without papers of any kind, I was challenging the authority and power of the nation-state. Though I was "inside" a particular country, I was moving "outside" its laws. I had moved into a lawless — or, as the Founding Fathers termed it, "natural" — area outside national sovereignty.

Like a foreign country, I had become suspect simply because no national law or regulation covered my actions.

Following the example of the millions of immigrants who had flooded into the United States in the late 19th and early 20th Centuries, I had made a free choice based on a body of law dating back to the Homestead Act of 1862. I had exercised my right to choose — or, in this case, give up — my nationality. According to the Expatriation Act of 1868, this was a "natural and inherent right." Yet the choice thrust me into a legal vacuum. My fundamental rights were no longer protected by the laws of any nation.

In the eyes of the nation-state, I no longer "existed."

On the other hand, by permitting me to give up my nationality, the United States had also done something quite profound. It had denied its exclusive sovereignty and, in the same stroke, had recognized the sovereignty of individual human beings.

Chapter 6

The Sources of Sovereignty

What is sovereignty, national or otherwise? In traditional terms, the sovereign is one who has rank or authority over another. In the distant past, the word referred most often to a deity or absolute ruler, the holder of supreme or ultimate power. Over the past century, however, the idea of sovereignty has shifted from the individual to the collective, from the ruler to the entire people.

Virtually all modern constitutions refer to "the people" as sovereign, or as the mandating authority for the constitution itself. "All public power in Sweden emanates from the people," says that country's statement of basic principles. Brazil's constitution begins the same way. In Greece, "popular sovereignty is the foundation of government." And under German law, the "dignity of man" is "inviolable"; its respect and protection is the "duty of all state authority." In Article 9, the Japanese Constitution even prohibits the state of belligerency. A study of national constitutions will quickly reveal their fundamental similarity. Authority is invariably derived from "the people," and, at least in theory, constitutions are designed to serve their sovereign people.

In essence, the exercise of personal sovereignty is the basis of authority for the social contract called government.

Let's say, for example, that you are alone on a desert island. You are citizen and government combined. You make the decisions and carry them out. But one day you spot a raft floating to shore, and I am on it. Now you face a choice: kill me or welcome me. If you kill me, you have further extended your sovereignty, judging me as an "undesireable alien" or even an "enemy" and then acting as executioner.

If you welcome me, on the other hand, it becomes "our" island. You have exercised your inalienable right to make a social contract with another human being. When we agree to act in a reasonable way toward one another, something ennobling and profound occurs: we become a community. As a community, we gain an added sovereignty, since this whole is greater than the sum of its two parts. Although we have lost absolute freedom, we have gained a new security. Simply put, your freedom ends where mine begins. And there lies the beginning of law and government.

So far, so good.

But most national constitutions also contain a crucial caveat. In some places it is called "national security," in others "public order." Whatever the label, it essentially overrules sovereignty and nullifies human rights. When human rights collide with national security, the result is typically outright violation, with disastrous consequences for any citizen in the way. Ultimately, security becomes a euphemism for aggression, an excuse for violence against nature and other living beings.

Describing the dilemma in blunt terms, former U.S. Secretary of State Dean Acheson once observed that law simply doesn't deal with "questions of ultimate power — power that comes close to the sources of sovereignty. . . . The survival of states is not a matter of law." Essentially, the social contract within an individual nation is a hostage of its inherent contradictions.

We are drawing closer to a basic paradox. The world's association of "sovereign" states — the United Nations — refers frequently to something called international law. Yet law stops at national frontiers, since a nation's authority cannot extend beyond either its constitutional limits or the spacial limits defined by its borders. Delegates from various nations talk about reaching beyond their own frontiers to achieve peace, and yet the same nations cling desperately to their claim of absolute sovereignty. And to do that, they routinely refuse to recognize the sovereign human — the source of their original authority.

A classic example of this paradox are the Nuremberg Principles, formulated by the International Law Commission of Jurists, and incorporated into "international" law by a resolution of the UN in 1950. The Principles state that "any person who commits an act which constitutes a crime under international law is responsible therefore and liable to punishment." Among the crimes are the planning or waging of a war "in violation of international treaties, agreements and assurances." But treaties and such between sovereign nations are totally outside popular control. How can someone be a party to treaty violations when he wasn't party to the treaty itself? Are individuals subject to international law? The Nuremberg Principles supposedly apply only to individuals, and yet in the International Court of Justice individuals have no standing.

This is about as just and sensible as a court, established by Mafia families to adjudicate their own nefarious activities, which only grants access to the families themselves — and only if each family agrees. Such a court would be a travesty, a mere smokescreen behind which the families preyed upon an innocent public with no power to appeal. If individuals can be held accountable for crimes that transcend national law, those who ought to be brought to justice under the Nuremberg Principles are most heads of state, the select few who have certain status under "international law." If the people are sovereign, however, then they too are responsible — even though they have little power at the moment and are usually denied standing. But in that case, a true world court would have built-in sanctions against individuals who violated world law. This is a matter of continuing debate in international legal circles.

For Americans, the Ninth Amendment to the Constitution provides additional evidence of this popular sovereignty. The Amendment recognizes unenumerated rights of natural endowment — inalienable rights that are beyond the jurisdiction of the government or courts. Clearly, the people are sovereign, not as merely national citizens but as human beings. The U.S. system of government is grounded solidly in the concept of natural rights. Government's purpose, at least in theory, is to protect people in their basic, natural rights, and ensure that they can hold their government to this end.

Humankind in turn represents the ultimate sovereign on planet Earth, the whole of which each of us is a part. Any government that refuses to recognize humanity as the ultimate sovereign is actually denying the source of its own authority. Plainly, no constitution can deny, inhibit or limit the sovereignty of humankind.

National order derives its authority from the sovereignty of the people within that limited community. It stands to reason, then, that world order derives its authority from those residing in that community — namely, citizens of the world.

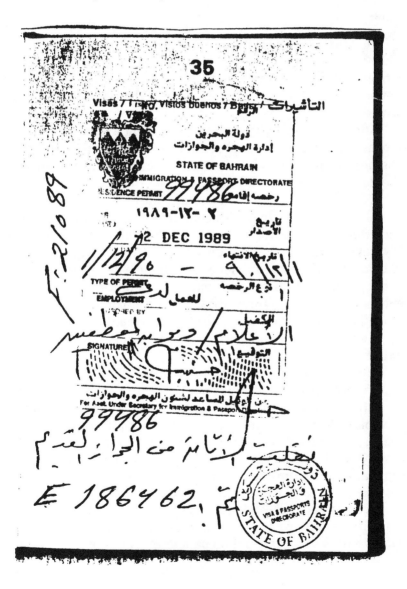

Chapter 7

Identity Found

Standing before a French bureaucrat in 1948, I saw my situation in much simpler terms than individual sovereignty versus the nation-state. Without papers, I was no longer "in" society. In fact, my very identity was suddenly in doubt. My papers were more valid than the person they represented.

After conferring with a superior, she sent me back to the U.S. Embassy to obtain a letter proving that they had taken away my passport. Letter in hand, I returned the next day. Now satisfied, she stamped it with an imposing seal.

"Now you exist," she said triumphantly.

Along with existence, she conferred a visa of three months and offered the hope that it might be extended. I was not grateful. My new credential verified only the fact that I was paperless. According to France, I did not exist without a document to prove it. But perhaps it was not my existence but France's that had been enhanced. I promptly threw the letter away. Three months later I faced the same bureaucrat and explained what I had done.

"I got rid of it," I said, "because it represents something that I didn't need to recognize."

"You ... don't ... recognize ... France?"

"France does not recognize me."

Although she began to grasp the absurdity of the situation, she coldly turned the matter over another office. She also revealed that she had been keeping track of my escapades through newspaper clippings. As the "First World Citizen" I had attracted some attention from the international press. No longer a mere paperless refugee, I had become a political celebrity.

Two days later, despite my celebrity status, the French government refused me permission to remain within its borders. I had two weeks to leave, but no papers and, apparently, no place

I could go. In essence, I had been told to live perpetually in international waters, seek asylum on another planet, die or go to jail. When August 27 arrived, I went to a police station and requested an extention, on the excuse that I needed a bit more time to arrange my departure to Luxembourg. The official was flexible but clear. I could stay until September 11.

Remain longer, he warned, and I would see the inside of a French prison.

There was no longer much choice. I had to take the bureaucratic bull by the horns. If I was going to battle bureaucracy with any hope of success, I would need documents of my own.

The first was a simple white paper — the United World Citizen International Identity Card. Only 1,000 copies were issued, and my own succeeded mainly in helping me to clarify my new identity. By creating papers and staking my claim to world citizenship, I was exercising individual sovereignty. This was the only way I could find to protect my human right to choose my own political allegiance.

Over the next five years several hundred thousand people joined me as World Citizens. They registered at the International Registry I founded in Paris and received more sophisticated identity cards, entering into a new and revolutionary social contract. Reclaiming their sovereignty, each of them turned his or her natural identity as a citizen of the world into a political fact. Together, they went further: they gave birth to a World Government.

Chapter 8

Four Levels of Identity

If population alone determined sovereignty, places like New York, Tokyo, London, Mexico City, and Shanghai would have a greater right to claim nation-state status than most of the countries in the UN. Over 90 nations have fewer people than Los Angeles. Obviously, neither population nor size determines national sovereignty.

Claims of sovereignty, enshrined in most constitutions, begin with "the people." If they are telling the truth, then the true sovereign is humanity. But that also means each human, the fundamental unit of humanity. This is the geo-dialectical key to world peace. As human beings, we communicate on four levels of Dynamic Identification. The first is one to One, the most intimate relationship we have with our spiritual nature. Our whole life is spent identifying with and identifying this dynamic.

The second is with the family. As we pass through life, our family takes many forms: biological, legal, social and spiritual. It is always an intimate group identification, the place where we apply our value system, where we test our strength and expose our weaknesses. The third level moves us beyond the family and into a personal area of immense variety. While stimulating co-operation and sharing, communication on this level also breeds fear, aggressiveness and distrust. Philosophy and attitudes often contradict the dynamic identifications established at the previous levels. Humans are pitted against each other. Scarcity thinking and unjust patterns of ownership are promoted. Often divisive, this level leads to warlike attitudes and finally to war itself. Alliances, treaties, and charters between sovereign states also stem from this dynamic identification, the political manifestation of the accumulated debris of war. Although we live in a "global village" of information, we are prisoners in exclusive "villages" called states. Virtually all governments express fear or paranoia of some enemy; for most this is the rationale for a suicidal arms race. Expressing its fear, government deprives its citizens of individual freedom in the name of security. The legal term for this is *Inter armes, silent legis*; or "Between armed states, the law is silent." When law is silent, humans become mere subjects of dictatorships, either overt or covert. This is the point at which communication between citizen and government breaks down. The nation-state itself becomes part of a dictatorial system of government.

The way out of this trap lies on the fourth level of Dynamic Identification. Holistic, or fourth level, values have been defined throughout human history. In the past, this level was the province of sages, prophets, poets, philosophers, artists and pirates. Before the technological and electronic breakthroughs of our age, each of these innovators demonstrated the concept of inalienable rights. They related the individual to his or her humanity, often under pressure from exclusive, third level regimes.

Today the key to re-establishing communication between citizen and government is available to everyone. Human rights, world law and world citizenship are fourth level expressions of a new and primal sovereignty. They recognize humanity and the individual human being. Through them we can retake control of our destiny, expressing the essence of the democratic principle.

Chapter 9

Bureaucratic Territory

You don't have to be a World Citizen to reclaim your sovereignty. But if you intend to exercise any sort of self-rule in your life, you'll have to teach yourself to deal effectively with bureaucrats and their paper-made labyrinths. You'll have to talk back, stay out of or escape from bureaucracy's grasp, and learn to use its raw power against itself.

After many years "outside" the big bureaucracy called the nation-state, I've unavoidably accumulated some expertise in this area. Most of my experience has been with national bureaucracies, those dealing with issues of travel, borders, and citizenship. The suggestions that follow, however, can be useful as well in dealing with other bureaus and officials.

Although I have been a stateless person and a World Citizen since 1948, my experiences are not as unique as you might at first assume. First of all, there are more than 350,000 World Citizens scattered around the world, people traveling with documents issued by the World Government that came into being after I began printing documents in 1948. And of course, there is a growing world population of stateless refugees. Nationalistic conflicts and rivalries erupting in wars have forced over 30 million people out of their homelands. Set adrift in a divided world of nations, these victims, most of them fleeing for safety, face a cruel identity crisis as they join what has been called the "nation of the nationless."

But even if you are not a stateless refugee, even if your identity as a national citizen is in no way threatened, at times you will feel as if your status affords little protection from degrading exploitation and the harrassment of anonymous bureaucrats and unconcerned officials. Like a casualty of war, you will find yourself lectured, herded and refused for no good reason. You will read regulations that make no sense, and face rules that contradict the regulations you just read. Trapped "inside" the sovereign domain of the system, you will feel dominated and persecuted, like a hostage in your own community.

These aren't just feelings. They are facts of life in the realm of arbitrary power. Particularly when we deal with national bureaucracies, which claim their legitimacy from the concepts of state sovereignty and national security, we are all potential hostages of the nation-state.

The primary tools that permit the continuous consolidation of this power are documents — forms, permits, letters, applications, cards, passports, and other varieties too numerous and enervating to list.

Over the years, my specialty has been passports due principally to being "outside" the whole frontier system. In the years since becoming a "stateless" person, I've consistently — and often dramatically — asserted the human right to travel freely as a citizen of the world. At countless borders, I have presented my own documents and explained my status as a World Citizen. I've challenged the authority of national governments, sometimes with remarkable results. Of course, I have seen the inside of many jails along the way, simply because I don't possess a passport issued by a national government. On the other hand, many countries have admitted me not merely as a visitor but as an honored guest. Many other World Citizens have had similar experiences.

But before we deal with the benefits and responsibilities of World Citizenship, let's consider a problem facing all citizens — bureaucracy.

Chapter 10

Learning the Language

When I face a border bureaucrat, I arrive well prepared. Normally, I'm well dressed and armed with a World Passport. My passport, a powerful symbol of the fact that we live in one world, explains in seven languages that I have the right to travel. Though the official may never have seen such a document before, it speaks his language, the language of the frontier.

If you want to neutralize a bureaucrat, you have to address him in terms he can understand. He may understand the truth. If he is a frontier guard, for example, he may realize that the frontier is a foolish illusion. He's trapped in an undignified, demeaning job that he may not believe in or even like. Yet he is paid, and so he does his job.

Usually, he does it without much enthusiasm. And he doesn't deal with theory. Like the machine he has been trained to be, he follows rules and handles documents. Presenting a passport — any passport — to a border bureaucrat is something he can easily understand. He knows the routine: take the passport and examine it.

If he's confused — for instance, if he's never seen your document before, he'll ask some questions.

"What kind of passport is this?" he might ask.

So you explain it to him. It's issued by the World Service Authority, based on specific articles in the Declaration of Human Rights. It's a human rights passport, you say.

He may not be convinced. "It's not valid," he tells you. "Of course, it is," you reply, and thus begin a dialogue to answer his questions. The document, usually the bureaucrat's refuge, has become your tool. Since it is your document, you know what it means. Its words and structure, which use the official's own language and logic, begin to neutralize his objections.

"Look on page 5," you tell him. "There's the validity date." The fact that it contains such a date enhances the document's legitimacy. Dates and numbers are the bureaucrat's talisman's. Each person he meets on the job must be related to some date or number. It is part of what he is paid to do. Give yourself a number and date, help him to fill in the blanks on his form, and you've begun the process of charming (or neutralizing) him.

He may still not be convinced. Though partially charmed, he may simply assume that his superiors or his government won't recognize your document.

At this point, your attitude becomes even more important. You must not only know what you're talking about, but convey an absolute certainty that you are right.

"Of course, you recognize my passport," you tell the confused official. "It's based on Article 13, Section 2 of the Universal Declaration of Human Rights."

Now you're speaking his language, but moving the dialogue beyond his level. Border bureaucrats, for example, seldom know more about the term "human rights" than how to spell it. Meanwhile, you appear quite confident that your document provides more than sufficient authority to pass through the bureaucrat's symbolic frontier. This approach may not always be enough. Later in this guide, you will find specific advice on what to do if a border official turns you down at first. For the moment, however, let's consider the border merely a symbol for any barrier you need to cross in the bureaucratic world. The keys are knowledge, proof, and confidence, along with a mastery of the language appropriate for the occasion.

And so, some simple rules.

Chapter 11

How to Overrule Bureaucracies: Ten Steps

1. Get Organized, Stay Organized.

If you know what you're talking about, you're always at an advantage in a bureaucratic exchange. The official, as part of the machine, knows little more than his narrow function and the regulations on which it is based.

When you ask questions, you shift the burden of responsibility. If the official plans to take some action, ask for the specific authority allowing him to do it. You don't have to accept excuses, like "the form says so." If the source of authority can be found, what date was it issued? Does it have a number? Who signed it? Is that person still in office or on the job?

If the official doesn't buckle by this time and decides to refuse you anyway, ask for the specific reason why. And get his or her name and rank. All bureaucrats have some classification, much like a military rank. Just asking for this information may win you a more favorable response. On the other hand, it may strain an already difficult relationship. Keep notes on all of this, including the bureaucrat's attitude toward you. He is supposed to remain cool and dispassionate, but if you do all of the above there's a high likelihood he'll go ballistic.

Whatever happens:

2. Stay Cool.

The worst thing you can do, at least at the ground level, is blow your top. Since you are right and he is wrong, the strongest response is to expose the truth without opposing the individual. Becoming emotional will only devalue what you have to say.

3. Go to the top.

Bureaucrats don't deal with us as human beings. They simply want us to fill out the form or provide the appropriate document, and then send it on to the next level. If you're having trouble at the bottom, however, you don't have to restrict yourself to his rigid chain of command. You can go right to the top.

This is especially true when you are acting in some way "outside" the system. When you're outside a chain of command, you have access to the entire chain. "A cat can look at a king," the saying goes. Well, if some low-level functionary turns you down, you can appeal to the president, prime minister or even king.

Sometimes the mere prospect of such an appeal, along with an appropriate document, is enough to force the bureaucrat at the bottom to back off. Of course, your document — if you're creating your own — must fit into his framework. It has to include your name and a number. It must be printed, with its text in several languages. And it should be laminated.

If your document meets the specifications, even if the bureaucrat has never seen it before, he'll look it over carefully and send his report up the chain of command. When you're "outside" the system, however, no one along the chain feels he has the authority to make a decision. Few systems can cope with an unfamiliar but convincing document.

Up and up it will go, landing finally on the desk of the person at the top of the chain. There, in most cases, it will be promptly forgotten. Meanwhile, back on the ground, you remain free.

4. Assume you are right.

A word to the wise may truly be sufficient. It is best to assume that when those with real authority learn of the rightness of your position, they will take the necessary steps to rectify the mistake. By calmly informing people that they are violating your rights, you are making them accomplices to a potential crime.

Even if he is not wise, no authority figure wants to be caught making a legal mistake. Faced with a potential violation and a confident accuser, even Immigration officials can be neutralized. My entry into the United States in 1950 is a case in point.

When I decided to return to the country of my birth, I knew I had the *Declaration of Human Rights* on my side. In attempting to define freedom of travel, the UN had affirmed "the right to leave any country." Clearly, if you leave a country, you're also entering one. But the UN delegates, all speaking for exclusive nations, could not say that outright. The question of what constitutes a person's "own country," or whether humans are actually born into the world itself rather than into some limited territory, was left unanswered. I had my own answer by then. My country was the world.

For the moment, however, I wanted to visit a territory known as the United States, and the embassy official I met said that, to do that, I would have to immigrate. He handed me a form.

Where it asked for my place of residence, I wrote my father's New York address. Filling the blank following "Desire to immigrate to," my answer was the same.

Looking the paper over, the bureaucrat was perplexed. "But you can't immigrate to your own residence," he said.

I replied, "I didn't say I was immigrating. You did. I'm just returning home."

"Home?" The word puzzled him. "But I thought you renounced your citizenship?"

"Yes, but I didn't renounce my home. After all, how could I?" Reviewing the form, he could find no logical solution. It was based on the mythology of national frontiers, while I lived in a united world without borders. Shrugging, he told me to come back the next day.

Doing so, I was given permission to immigrate under a "non quota" program. After 40 years I still haven't located it in any statute, and no State Department official has ever mentioned the contradiction.

5. Keep them informed.

When you decide to go topside, it's vital to keep everyone informed, however remotely involved they may appear. Let the underlings know that you're communicating with their superiors, extending as far up the chain as you can go. Going public, both within a bureaucracy and beyond its boundaries, can make all the difference.

When Yusuf Kaya, a Turkish resident of the United States, found himself stranded in West Germany, the power of information to neutralize an iron-clad bureaucracy and re-assert a person's threatened identity became crystal clear. Hospitalized with a heart attack in the fall of 1972, Kaya's passport expired before he could return to his U.S. residence. The Turkish authorities hesitated to issue him a new one. In a fit of anger, Kaya unilaterally renounced his nationality. Though he obtained a World Registration Card and passport from the World Service Authority, presenting them to the Commissioner of Foreign Police did not bring a favorable response. The ex-Nazi behind the desk was not impressed.

"These are totally invalid," the man said, warning Kaya that if he remained in Germany beyond the end of the year he'd be taken into custody.

As the end of December approached, Kaya faced a grim future. The Turks, undoubtedly suspicious about his act of renunciation, were more inclined to punish him than help out. And the Germans, who viewed Turks as no more than slave-wage "guest workers," were positively unsympathetic.

The only hope that remained was the World Government that had issued his rejected documents. His lawyer told him they were fraudulent; after all, he argued, there is no World Government. But with Turkey and West Germany conspiring to strip Kaya of his identity, could his new allegiance help him to reassert it? We began by writing to Herr Renner, the German bureaucrat at the bottom of the chain. On World Government stationery, we explained that his expulsion order violated the Human Rights Declaration. Turning the tables, we warned that Renner's false allegation about Kaya's passport was itself prejudicial and overstepped his authority. Refering to both human rights and German law, we urged him to reverse his decision. Copies of the letter were sent by registered mail to Chancellor Willy Brandt, UN Secretary General Waldheim, and Kaya.

Although this first volly didn't completely neutralize the bureaucrat, it did impress Kaya's lawyer. A subsequent phone call by the lawyer resulted in a 30 day extension to study the increasingly unusual case.

The next problem was the Turkish government, which now wanted its ex-citizen back in its clutches. The stakes were getting higher. If Kaya was forced to return to Turkey now, he could end up in prison or facing a firing squad.

The next letter went to Willy Brandt. Reviewing the case and citing the vital importance of human rights, we asked the Chancellor to intervene. At the end was a veiled warning. If no confirmation was received by January 27, "We shall be obliged to take whatever measures we feel necessary to expose this situation for the public record." Copies again went to Waldheim, Renner and Kaya.

By January 30, no reply had been received. The only choice left was to defend Kaya in person. With only my World Passport to protect me from the jaws of the nation that threatened to chew up Yusuf Kaya, I drove to the Franco-German frontier. The sleepy West German guard barely looked up as I waved and drove through.

Upon finding Kaya, I learned that his lawyer was sitting on the matter, still unsure whether the claims and papers were legitimate. My presence apparently made the difference.

The case was clear-cut, I explained. It was a matter of national law regarding a so-called foreigner versus human rights and world law. "Perhaps you don't realize the profound legal implications," I went on. "If Mr. Kaya isn't competently represented by you as a citizen of our government, I'll see to it that you bear the full brunt of responsibility along with the West German government."

The lawyer had heard enough. The situation, as well as the documents, might be unusual, he said, "but I can appreciate they have a certain relevancy to his basic rights." With that, he assured us that Kaya's deportation could and would be prevented.

In the end, Kaya remained in West Germany with full residence and working rights. Sometime later, when he decided to marry a Romanian woman, he contacted World Government again. This time he needed a marriage license; the Germans were refusing to marry a "stateless Turk" and a Romanian refugee. His government — World Government — was delighted to oblige.

6. Keep track of the paper.

Yusuf Kaya's story demonstrates the results you can get by keeping people informed. In that case, the object became convincing a lawyer that the cause was legitimate enough to do his job. The case also underlines the importance of a paper trail in the bureaucratic land of documents.

When writing to officials, don't skimp on copies. Send them to high government officials, key minsters, the bureaucrat directly involved in the problem or violation, and, if travel rights or citizenship are involved, to the Secretary-General of the UN. Equally important is the use of registered mail, which guarantees delivery, underlines the seriousness of your communication, and makes it clear that you know they've been informed. If your letters, spelling out the situation and the legal basis of your request, are circulated to the appropriate places, no one along the chain of command is likely to get in the way. Faced with a legal conundrum and the prospect of bad publicity, they will often opt to give you what you want.

When 12 students detained in Hamburg's city jail contacted the World Service Authority in 1974, one well-phrased letter was sufficient. The young men — from Cameroon, Ghana, Egypt, British Honduras, South Africa and Tunisia — were facing deportation. For many of them, returning home meant imprisonment. For the Cameroonians, whose government had changed hands while they studied abroad, deportation might mean death. Up until then, the German bureaucracy had been deaf to their pleas.

After issuing their World Passports, we wrote to then Chancellor Helmut Schmidt. Arbitrary detention, particularly when potential deportees face extreme hardship, is a direct violation of both the Human Rights Declaration and the International Covenant on Civil and Political Rights, we explained.

"You will appreciate," the letter went on, "that Article I, Part I of the International Covenant on Civil and Political Rights, recognizing the right of self-determination of political status by individuals, affirms thus the inherent right of sovereign choice by the humans concerned. The right of the individual therefore to commit his or her civil and political allegiance to World Government is herein sanctioned."

After several more legalistic flourishes, the letter closed with the usual appeal to justice, fundamental rights and German law. Copies went to Waldheim, the head of the prison, our legal contact in the U.S. (who had recently become Chief Justice of another institution for World Citizens, the World Court of Human Rights), and the 12 World Citizens awaiting deportation.

The reaction was immediate. Someone in the federal government of West Germany had realized that many hot issues were involved. Apparently not ready to grapple with several overlapping controversies — human rights vs. national law, Africans vs. Europeans, blacks, vs. whites, and national government vs. world government — the unidentified but apparently highly placed official gave the order to release the men. Within days 12 detainees had become legal residents. Given the anonymity of bureaucratic power, it is difficult to say with complete certainty why the government caved in. It may well have been the implied threat to expose human rights violations buried in the careful legalistic language. Whatever the main reason, the fact that someone was monitoring the case, and was apparently capable of taking steps to keep it alive, certainly didn't hurt.

7. Find the right words.

If you are going to talk to bureaucrats, you need the right vocabulary. It's not simply a matter of being polite, though that is usually appropriate. You must understand bureaucratic protocol, and how to write a letter that both impresses, threatens and cajoles. When communicating on paper, find the proper form of greeting and conclusion. When is it "Excellency," "Your Grace," or "Your Honor," and when do you write plain "Sir"? Nations and bureaucracies are a grab-bag of people with titles you can ill afford to confuse. A cat can talk to a king alright, but he won't get far by saying "meow." If it's an ongoing exchange, make sure to refer to "previous correspondence," and send photocopies when appropriate. Just as officials try to divert you with vagueries, you can tangle them in the history of your case and rationale.

When defending your rights, make sure you can define them — whether they're in state law, your constitution, or the *Universal Declaration of Human Rights*. Whenever possible, take a copy of the document along to the meeting.

Not everyone can use language with equal facility. You may be shy, unfamiliar with legalese, or simply not that articulate.

Don't worry. You are right, after all, and you can lean on the printed words that back up your case. You can also demand that the bureaucrat define them, if you're not sure how. They're supposed to be "experts," after all. You should, of course, present your basic case, using the key words that apply to the situation. When it is a question of travel or nationality, for example, a key word is always "citizen." From the latin word "civitas," it refers to any body of people living under the same law. The citizens might be part of a community, nation-state, or even larger group. Defining social and political rights within a particular human community, it is a word of sovereign power, but also relative and limited to those with equal civic rights.

As a citizen dealing with a state or nation, you are usually attempting to assert particular "rights." Here is a word that everyone uses but very few really understand. Rights may be granted under a national constitution, or they may transcend it and be "inalienable" — that is, incapable of being transferred to any other person or authority. In fact, humans do have rights that go beyond mere legal guarantees, rights that belong to us precisely because we are human. These "natural rights" are based on our ability to reason and our capacity for moral choice. When you claim "I've got my rights" in a society cluttered with bureaucratic rules and conflicting legal theories, "natural rights" are usually the kind to which you are referring, whether you know it or not. They may also often be your last refuge. Natural rights are the bedrock of freedom, necessary for the cultivation and expression of our highest qualities.

By turning to natural rights, then, you are saying that other rights and obligations are tentative and can be examined, that our forms of government, our social institutions, are open to criticism and change. By putting "nature" in front of rights, you claim that any and all institutions must justify themselves.

In all societies, the great jurist William Blackstone explained, the individual surrenders some "natural liberty" and "in consideration of receiving the advantages of mutual commerce obliges himself to conform to those laws which the community has thought proper to establish." In short, not all natural rights can be exercised within the laws of a specific community.

But we humans also have "human rights," which are enumerated in documents like the Universal Declaration. The phrase itself betrays a subtle contradiction: Rights are limited and relative, but human is a universal and unitive word, linking the social, biological and spiritual. By putting "human" in front of "rights," we move the realm of freedom beyond a political framework defined by a limited community. Perhaps the most universal and unitive word of all, however, is "world." It encompasses the Earth and the heavens, humanity and all its affairs. It is immense and holistic, complete and total, opening out into the cosmos. When dealing with citizenship and our rights, it is a word that makes a profound difference.

At one time it made sense to cling to limited notions such as nationalism and national citizenship. For many immigrants, giving up citizenship in one place and seeking it in another was a door to increased freedom and security. It was also the exercise of a fundamental right — the right to choose one's allegiance to a government.

Today, however, the old logic no longer holds up. In a wartorn and ecologically endangered world, national citizenship clearly provides no security. Our basic problems have become global, and jumping from one national identity to another hardly helps. When you put "world" in front of "citizen," however, you expand your rights and options. Your framework becomes global, and you begin to re-empower yourself as a human being.

It would be misleading to claim that merely explaining these terms and concepts to a border guard will be enough, by itself, to get you through. Like any bureaucratic encounter, the outcome is a matter of both content and form, as well as timing and your own demeanor. But your ability to speak the bureaucrat's language, understand his terminology and, to the greatest extent possible, force him to use your definitions, will make a crucial difference between merely stating and actually claiming your rights.

8. Make yourself look good.

As humans we are all equal. But to an official, we are what our documents, letters and appearance imply we are. A perfect argument, if presented sloppily, or by someone who is unconventionally clad, will very likely fall on deaf ears.

Our success in helping people travel with documents identifying them as World Citizens rests, to a certain extent, on the fact that they "look" like what they are. As trivial as it may seem, surface impressions count. Thus, never handwrite anything you send to a bureaucrat. Always type, or use a computer.

If you don't know how to prepare an official, impressive-looking letter, there are many basic manuals that can help. It doesn't hurt, of course, to have some nice stationery or to be part of some organization. If you don't have an organization, you might consider creating one that suits your purposes. And since words clearly do have power, pick a name that enhances your image while making a point. When setting up the administrative side of World Government, for instance, we decided on the name, World Service Authority (WSA). In addition to the all-encompassing nature of the world, we were offering "service," what government really ought to be, and claiming "authority" to do it. It's doubtful we would have gotten as far if the name had been Wonderful Stateless Activists.

Equally important as your presentation on paper is your presentation in person. If you travel internationally, no doubt you've noticed how border officials select those they intend to favor with the "full treatment." It may be one's insecure demeanor, or the nervous answer given to a routine question. Or it might just be a question of wardrobe. Bureaucrats are trained to pay attention to such details, and in a strange way, to turn their petty prejudices into criteria for judgements.

If you know this, on the other hand, why not use their tunnel vision to reach your goal. In 1956, for example, my goal was to go to India and visit a guru. It was to be my first trip out of the United States after returning in 1950. Before I left I knew that, as a stateless traveler, I would often be confronted by uniforms and police. When you visit most countries, people in uniform are the first ones you meet. Two ideas came to mind.

By this time, we had established a World Government of World Citizens. I'll say more about that later. But like any government, we obviously needed our own police — in this case, a world police force. The second, related idea had to do with the mental set of uniformed bureaucrats: one thing they certainly respect is another person in uniform. Putting the two ideas together, I set about making a uniform for our new police force. Emblazoned on it was the name — Sovereign Order of World Guards. Just think about those words!

In April, 1956, I landed in Bombay, carrying a World Passport and wearing my new uniform. When the immigration officer, a brisk young man, reviewed my document and looked me over, he didn't know what to do. Since I had flown from New York, that meant I had some money at least. But I had handed him an unusual passport and wore a uniform he had never seen before. What would he do?

A knock at the door broke the tension. Poking in his head, a reporter asked, "I wonder if you would care to say a few words to the *Times of India*, Mr. Davis?"

"Just as soon as I am cleared here," I replied.

That did it. Giving me a nervous smile, the immigration officer eagerly grabbed a rubber stamp, and stamped my visa with a permit to enter.

My World Passport had passed its first test. But the visit was at least partially sanctioned by the press. Since the media transcend most frontiers, that came as no surprise. Looking back, however, I know my uniform also played a part. On other occasions it has done even more: it has saved me from jail.

In 1957, for instance, a guard in the Egyptian Embassy in Iran was told to arrest me for attempting to claim asylum there. As he approached, however, he noticed my uniform. It was better pressed than his. When he was about three feet away, I opened my coat and displayed a shiny badge. The idea that I was in uniform — and even had a badge — was just too much for him. The man turned white and fled. He couldn't bring himself to arrest another man in uniform.

9. Set a deadline.

An open-ended request to a high official is an invitation to forget all about it. On the other hand, a clear and definite time limit, especially a short one, is a warning to take notice. A generous time limit to correct a bureaucratic foul-up is about two weeks. When the issue is urgent, two days is not too little. Remember, you are the injured party. Your deadline is one way of underlining that fact. To reinforce the importance of your deadline, add an ultimatum. No one likes ultimatums, of course, but a deadline without consequences is merely a date. After all, we're not dealing with close friends here.

Your ultimatum can be somewhat abstract, of course. You

might say, for instance, that if the situation is not rectified within two weeks, "we will not be responsible for the consequences." Writing on behalf on Yusuf Kaya, I warned all concerned that we would "be obliged to take whatever measures we feel necessary to expose this situation" if Kaya was not allowed to remain in Germany. If you do plan a specific action, give them a taste of what lies ahead, without providing too many specifics.

In any case, you will probably want some sort of apology, perhaps a return of funds, and restitution of whatever may have been taken from you.

Setting a deadline, giving an ultimatum, and demanding that things be set aright are part of claiming your rights. These strong actions indicate your self-respect and your confidence in the correctness of your position. When a bureaucrat is unsure of how to resolve a case, intimidation may weigh on both sides of the scale. If you are firm, but also polite and show some respect for the humanity of the official, the combination can often tip things in your favor.

10. Remain firm.

Even if you do everything right, favorable results may not come quickly. They may not meet your deadline, or appear impressed with your arguments, ability to speak their language, your letterhead or your dress. Instead they may be counting on time and your lack of resolve. Most people will bluff about taking action; only a few are ready to actually follow through.

Having come this far, however, you owe it to yourself to stay the course. If dialogue has proven ineffective, action is next. The form of action bureaucrats like least is exposure. You know their names, and have copies of letters sent and returned. It may be time to tell the world.

It may even be time to camp on the top dog's doorstep. When he asks what you plan to do, refer him to previous correspondence. You've laid the groundwork. You've been reasonable and patient. You've even warned him you won't be responsible for the consequences.

It's his move — but it has become your game.

Chapter 12

A World Citizen Comes Home

Returning from India in 1957, I often found it necessary to use creative techniques in order to neutralize bureaucrats. Claiming asylum in the Egyptian Embassy in Iran, for instance, was my way of dealing with Iran's refusal to extend my visa. Unfortunately, it didn't work, and despite intimidating a policeman with my badge and uniform, I was eventually removed and forced to board a KLM flight.

But Iran's power to expel me did not mean that I was powerless. In fact, my status as a World Citizen gave me the ability to produce international convulsions — at least as long as I was prepared to stand firm. From Iran I was flown to Saudi Arabia, where I refused to get off the plane. From there they flew me to Pakistan, a place I had only recently left. Again refusing to disembark, I demanded a flight to my actual destination — Germany— and got it.

But Germany, it turned out, didn't want me either, and forwarded me to Holland, KLM's home base, where I was turned over to the police. Facing yet another man in uniform, I presented my passport for Dutch inspection.

"This is not a valid passport," he said. "You cannot stay in Holland."

"But you brought me to Holland," I answered. "Do you think I want to be here? Did I ask to come here?"

When they refused to let me make a phone call, I gave them five minutes to change their mind. For two days I had been flown around the world against my will. Now I was going to be put in jail. The time limit up, I reached up and pulled down the curtains covering the windows. Shocked guards eventually "subdued" me, and I was sent to the Amsterdam Prison. There I asked for the charge. They said I was just "in custody . . . a guest of the Queen."

A week later KLM flew me back to the U.S. Upon arrival I again refused to disembark. Within minutes the plane filled up with New York policemen. Photographers followed, shooting pictures of me and the police.

When a KLM official asked what I wanted, I handed him my passport and asked him to have Immigration accept it. After my experience in Holland, I wasn't planning to leave the plane without knowing what lay in store for me.

Five minutes later he was back with the news. "They refuse," he said, adding that I would soon be flying back to Holland again. "So be it," I said, my heart pounding.

What would happen next? I wondered. If I didn't get off in Holland, would they fly me back to Iran, then bundle me off to Pakistan and finally India? And then what? Nehru would probably order me back to New York. I had given him a World Passport, but that didn't mean he would support my cause. The merry-go-round might continue indefinitely. A half hour later two tough-looking Immigration men marched up and looked me in the eye.

"Okay, Davis, you're free," one said.

"That's right," I replied.

"No, I mean you're free. You can go."

After checking their credentials, I asked why.

"Ain't it clear? Free is free. We're freeing you."

"When did you jail me?"

"Listen, Davis, I'm not here to argue with you. I'm here to tell you what's what."

"All right," I said, "just what is what?"

"We're gonna parole you."

I laughed.

"Yeah, like the Hungarians. Special law. We're just following orders."

Realizing that acceptance of such a status would leave me with no access to the courts or other legal recourse, I declined the offer. Clearly irritated, they retreated to the pilot's section for a conference. When they returned, I offered to enter the United States on one condition.

"Yeah, what's that?" asked the cigar-chewing inspector.

"No conditions."

They exchanged glances, and decided to accept.

When I finally reached the Immigration section, it was deserted. I passed through like a wraith. At the end was a knot of journalists. "Why did you give in?" one asked.

"Who told you that?"

"The Immigration inspector," he explained. "He said you even signed parolee papers."

The phony story had already gone out over the Associated Press wire. I told them the truth, and eventually both versions received press in Europe. Immigration had succeeded, however, in making sure its story was the only one heard at home.

Trapping by their own rules and unwilling to deal with the true implications of my claim to World Citizenship, these border bureaucrats had resorted to deception. Still, I had neutralized them. And after a long and winding trip, with my World Passport and principles intact, I had come home.

11

Visas / Visas / Vistos buenos / Визы / التأشيرات /
se / Vizoj

Nº 1.41   A/O

VISA

Valable pour :
Geldig voor : Benelux/
Valid for :

Délivré le / Afgegeven op / Issued on .... Berlin

Ce visa est valable pour
Dit visum is geldig voor .... 1 .... mois/jours
This visa is valid   maanden/dagen
                                                         months/days

à partir du : 15.9.33/ de la date de la première entrée
vanaf   / de datum van eerste binnenkomst
from   / the date of first entry

pour un plusieurs voyage(s)
voor een/meerdere reis(zen)
for a single/several journey(s)

Première entrée avant
Eerste binnenkomst voor
First entry before

Durée de séjour ininterrompu   mois/jours
Duur ononderbroken verblijf   maanden/dagen
Duration of uninterrupted stay   months/days

Attention ! Faites estampiller votre passeport à la frontière
Opgelet !   Paspoort aan de grens laten afstempelen
Attention ! Passport to be stamped at the frontier

Taxe perçue

Chapter 13

Transcending Nationalism

All organized systems exist in dynamic tension between entropy and negentropy — that is, between chaos and order. Applying this concept to the human world, both tendencies are obvious and in many ways troubling. Faced with conflicts between individuals and nations, an information revolution, and a breakdown of traditional values, most societies today impose impersonal rules and rigid boundaries. Bureaucracies are modern society's way of imposing categories and regulating human nature; they are structures intended to maintain order and rationalize control. Their central values are anonymity, secrecy, and efficiency — although large bureaucracies are in practice grossly inefficient. Information is their fuel, refined into documents and processed by bureaucrats. Ultimately, they exist in order to perpetuate themselves.

Although some bureaucracies, such as the post office, do have essentially service-oriented functions, all require some sacrifice of freedom by their users or prisoners. The more expansive a bureaucracy's charge, the more freedom one may potentially lose. National bureaucracies, of course, require the greatest sacrifices of all — and promise the largest rewards.

In the 20th Century, it has become apparent that the natural rights of humanity are not protected by the national bureaucracies called nation-states. On the contrary, they assault freedom while simultaneously posing enormous risks to our survival. National "order" risks global "chaos."

When you talk back to a bureaucrat, however, you add a new ingredient — the uniqueness of the human being. You also imply that freedom should take precedence over rules, particularly if the rules defy justice and violate natural or human rights. When the bureaucrat you confront represents a national government, you are taking a stand for individual sovereignty and your natural rights as a human being. In doing so, you place yourself at the threshold of a new allegiance — to humanity and the world.

***

Before the industrial age and the electronic revolution, the mechanical barriers of geography restricted the boundary of our allegiance to, at most, the nation. Governments operated and histories were written from a distinctly non-global perspective. Loyalty to the feudal prince or, later, the sovereign king was direct and absolute. But beginning with the telegraph, first used in 1844, all that changed. From the start, it was clear that advances in communication technology would have a profound impact on society as a whole. The emergence of "telegraphic news" was trumpeted as "the annihilation of space." James Gordon Bennett of the *New York Herald* claimed that electronic communication had begun the evolution of a "new species of consciousness." The transatlantic cable, completed in 1858, was billed as the "eighth wonder of the world."

With lines of communication linking relatively isolated social units, our thoughts could be shared almost instantly from a distance. Personal, direct contact was no longer necessary. Politically, this marked the true birth of indirect representation. Along with that came the increased popularity of the notion that the governed should have a voice in government. Democracy, kindled in the context of rising expectations, inflamed revolutions from east to west, north to south. At the same time, however, a paradox was also born. While the essence of democracy is universal participatory decision-making, the essence of national sovereignty is exclusivity and the non-participation of those outside the national boundary. "Citizens" with rights "belonged" to the nation; everyone else was a "foreigner" or "alien." Just when human beings were discovering that it was possible to communicate globally, nationalism threw up border after border, restricting contact and defining the boundaries between us. Although the first manifestation of modern nationalism occurred in 17th Century England, it became dominant only after the American and French revolutions. By the mid-19th Century, the nation-state was the primary actor on the world stage, defining itself as sovereign — that is, accepting no superior authority. Nation-states also claimed complete ownership and control of their defined territories and the populations living within them. Each state was held to be independent and absolute. The largest sought to maximize their own power, often by expanding their territory.

Qualities were and still are attached to various national labels, often justifying violence and aggression toward the "foreigners." Humanity, already divided into "Americans," "Russians," "Chinese" and "Iranians," was further categorized as good and bad, noble and barbaric, superior and inferior. This stereotyping, a grotesque outgrowth of nationalism, has continued in the last years of the 20th Century with phrases such as the "evil empire" (the Soviet Union until Gorbachev) and the "great Satan" (the United States, according to Muslim fundamentalists), and the demonization of Arabs as irrational terrorists. When the opponent is characterized as a "monster," any response — even genocide — can be rationalized.

During the past two hundred years, political power has been channeled into the rigid framework of nationalism. Those who have attempted to identify with humanity as a whole have been belittled as idealists, utopians, sentimental humanitarians, impractical moralists, or simply crackpots. Prior to this century, the only true "citizens" of the world were pirates, those "stateless" wanderers who sailed freely on the open seas. They have recently been replaced by multinational executives, modern-day pirates and "citizens" of the corporate world. At the same time, however, electricity and electronics have eliminated the barriers of time and distance. The world has become one community. As Marshall McLuhan explained so persuasively, dialogue has been reconstituted on a global scale. In the new "global village," the concerns of others pour in continuously. "We have become," he wrote, "irrevocably involved with, and responsible for, each other." The profound developments we have witnessed — revolutions in technology, electronics, nuclear power, and space exploration — demonstrate dramatically the inadequacies of the nation-state. Indeed, the nation-centered way of "solving" problems has become the problem.

***

Today each of us is the focus of global input. War in the Middle East raises oil prices everywhere. A nuclear accident in the Soviet Union can mean leukemia for a baby in Ohio. The dumping of radioactive waste off the coast of Florida can result in radioactive fish off the coast of France, Britain, or Spain. Everything happens at once. Everything happens to everyone. This is perhaps the most awesome fact of any century.

But what about the output? Shouldn't that also be global? The logic is clear: in our "global village," each individual should have the ability to participate in the world-at-large. The human body is an apt anology. In our bodies, each cell is linked to the whole by a nervous system directly connected to the human computer — our brain. For this remarkable coordinating mechanism to respond to a specific threat, it must receive instant feedback from ·damaged cells. As a "government" of the body, it considers both the individual and common good — the cell and the whole.

Government ought to function as humanity's brain, fulfilling the needs of the individual and the entire organism. This is precisely what the technological revolution of our century makes possible: instantaneous input and output for each human and for all humanity. For the first time in human history, global institutions can take their rightful place.

World citizenship, the main focus of this book, is a dynamic and imperative political identity that relinks the conceptual and moral value of the individual human being with the true social and economic organization of the planetary community. It expresses both the innate and inalienable sovereignty of each human and the overall sovereignty of the entire species. Meeting the criteria for both ethical and ethnical politics, it also suggests a plan of ongoing political action at all levels of society, from local to global.

In centuries past, national citizenship had to be taught, learned and experienced. Certainly, this process produced great turmoil and challenged the social norms of the period. Similarly, as we approach the 21st Century, world citizenship must be taught, learned and experienced.

Thinking, feeling and acting globally is virtually without precedent in recorded history. Until the age of high technology, only a few prophets managed this feat. But faced with the threat of destruction, through our violence against each other and the environment, we must all become prophets. Through world citizenship, we can rise above the "left" and "right" of nationalistic politics, making functional the perennial values which unite us all. Allegiance to humanity rather than an exclusive nation integrates the fundamental truth of science and religion: the world is one living whole.

Once this is accepted, it becomes far easier to relate to ourselves and to others in a dynamic way. With the opening of the Nuclear Age, we took a quantum leap in power. Now our political concepts must catch up. Making the leap from national to world citizenship is the major change in social consciousness that lies ahead.

Crossing Frontiers

Chapter 14

State of the Nation-State

"As nations are torn apart and restructured, as instabilities and threats of war erupt, we shall be called upon to invent wholly new political forms or 'containers' to bring a semblance of order to the world — a world in which the nation-state has become, for many purposes, a dangerous anachronism."
— Alvin Toffler, *The Third Wave*

A headline in the *Washington Post* posed a provocative and important question for the 1990s: IS THE NATION-STATE HEADED FOR THE DUSTBIN OF HISTORY? With supranational organizations and ethnic nationalist movements pulling the world in two conflicting directions, the *Post* surmised in November 1990 that notions of sovereignty and nationhood may be transformed in the near future.

Though geo-political "experts" aren't ready yet to list the nation-state as a terminal patient, few are optimistic, and most admit that global economic and political problems will inevitably "erode" national sovereignty. The symptoms of decline are difficult to ignore. Consider the following:

- The functions of the European Economic Community, other regional groupings of nations, and even the United Nations are rapidly expanding.
- There is general agreement that global action is the only way to deal with problems such as environmental pollution, drug trafficking, human rights abuses, and terrorism.

- The disputes in virtually every world trouble spot can be traced in part to defects in the nature of various nation-states. Most of the countries in conflict were born in this century and owe their existence to the collapse of the Ottoman, Hapsburg, British and French empires.
- The concept of "nation-state" is often a contradiction in terms. States are legalistic entities; nations are groups sharing a culture, language, religion, or history. Some legal "states" — the United States, Canada, Switzerland, Sri Lanka — are not "nations" but rather "multinational" states. Some nations — Kurds, Palestinians, Armenians, Crees — have no state. In fact, there are very few places where the two concepts come together.
- The world's major national economies are inextricably linked. When it's cold on Tokyo's stock market, London, Frankfurt and New York feel the chill.
- Member nations of NATO have already surrendered substantial powers in the area of defense. If currency and foreign policy become supranational concerns, control of the military will follow.
- Even the unpredictable movements for self-determination, autonomy, independence and reunification across borders that are underway within many existing nation-states are related to the global trend. Ethnic, religious and political conflicts represent awkward attempts to resolve deep-rooted identity questions produced by the century-long dominance of nation-states.

The contradictions confronting the existing system are enormous. The leaders of virtually every nation on the planet are trying desperately to maintain a fictitious "national unity" in the face of global trends and the revolutionary power of communication technology. Long before the Berlin wall came down, television demolished most of the national "walls" dividing people around the world. As predicted more than a century earlier, instantaneous communication truly has eliminated space as a barrier. For the first time in human history we have been able, literally, to "see" one another from opposite ends of the globe.

Of course, the first things noticed in the "global village" are the differences between us — cultural and racial divisions, disparities in health, wealth and basic conditions. But beyond this level is a more fundamental area of unity. As fellow citizens of this "village," we cannot help but notice what we share: our humanity, our endangered planet, and our status as prisoners of an anachronistic geo-political system.

As a consequence of this eye-opening experience it is no wonder that many of us ask: What good is the existing system? Do our leaders really know what they're doing? Do our institutions work? Why do the groups we view as our enemies and friends keep changing? And who or what is the real enemy anyway? Are nations capable of producing anything but war and waste? Are they worth saving? And if not, what do we put in their place?

11

Visas / I ioas / Vistos buenos / Визы / التأشيرات
ظع / Vizoj

HIS MAJESTY'S GOVERNMENT
ROYAL NEPALESE LIAISON OFFICE
HONG KONG

Category: _____ TRANSIT
40528   2 MAY 90
No:_____ Date:_____
Good for *Single* entry to Nepal
within 3 months of date hereof and stay
for 30 days if passport remains valid.
Fee: PAID / GRATIS

ROYAL NEPALESE LIAISON OFFICER, HONGKONG

Chapter 15

Allegiance to Insecurity

"... the world's present system of sovereign nations can lead only to barbarism, war and inhumanity ..."

— Albert Einstein

Before passing judgment on the nation-state system, we ought to define what it is. Historically, it is an outgrowth of feudalism. Only two centuries ago there were no more than nine so-called "sovereign nations." Geographically vast, these territories absorbed smaller areas — usually by violent means — and forced the resolution of lesser conflicts.

As popular revolutions threw off the yokes of princes and kings, more nations were born. During the same period, however, the most powerful nation-states became empires. Absorbing more and more territory, they arbitrarily began drawing borders in other parts of the world. Most of the borders for the nations of Africa were drawn at the Berlin Conference in 1884. For the countries of the Middle East, nationhood came with the collapse of the Ottomon empire; dividing the spoils, France and Britain drew artificial border lines that have caused conflicts in the region ever since. It is indeed ironic that what was initially a force for uniting small socio-political units became a system promoting global anarchy and war.

In 1900, there were still under 50 nation-states. By 1980, the number was over 160. And unless this trend is dramatically reversed, the world will have over 200 exclusive nation-states by the year 2000. Each will claim ownership of an arbitrarily defined section of the Earth's surface, as well as control of the people who happen to live within its borders. Each will have the sovereign right to wage war. Despite all efforts of "supranational" institutions, it will be legal for any nation to literally decimate portions of the planet as long as the appropriate protocols have been followed.

A world of nation-states is essentially a lawless, anarchic world in which conflict is the defining political and social force. For the nation, "national security" is another word for repression. War is a way to protect the "common welfare," often by destroying it. Environmental degradation is defined as merely a "trade off" for progress. And "human services," managed by government and dominated by a repressive ethic, are programs that quite often promote moral and social disintegration. Leaders are commonly liars and criminals; commercial institutions are machines that market violence for profit. In the nation-state, the social contract called "national citizenship" becomes a collective suicide pact. We simply don't know when we'll be asked to die — or for what.

What we do know is that the nation demands allegiance; in fact, it considers citizens its subjects. "Citizens" may owe allegiance, but they also receive protection that enhances their security, and are the source of their government's authority. "Subjects," on the other hand, are controlled arbitrarily either by a personal sovereign — whether a king, dictator, or sheik, or by a power elite outside their control. Thus, whether you live in a so-called "free" country or in a dictatorship, national citizenship is actually a form of imprisonment. The system itself is the prison, and national borders are the bars. The more we know, the less attractive this arrangement becomes. But can the nation-state at least deliver the true security it promises? Can it guarantee the first human right — life itself? Twenty million war-related deaths since the end of World War II provide a clearcut answer. In fact, even the most powerful nations cannot promise that a nuclear war won't begin "accidentally," or that they won't start it. If that sounds extreme, consider: even in our "post-Cold War" world the United States declines to promise that it will not use nuclear weapons first in some future conflict. According to the International Institute for Strategic Studies, "the political-military system that has more or less kept global order since World War II is breaking down and nothing is in sight to replace it." Big nations can no longer keep smaller nations in line. With technology provided by the industrial nations, some developing nations already have truly awesome military strength. But many of these have no stake in the "international order" created by their suppliers. In such an anarchic world community, today's friend is the nation that aids in dealing with a current enemy. In reality, status as a friend or enemy is more circumstantial than ideological. The harsh truth is that a nation, though it may suffer, can at least survive without many friends. What it absolutely requires is an enemy.

Chapter 16

The Passport Swindle

"PASSPORT: Authorization to pass from a port or leave from a country, or to enter and pass through a country; safe-conduct, granted usually with defined limitations of destination, time and purpose; but gradually extended in use until it now means a document issued by competent authority, granting permission to the person specified in it to travel, and authenticating his right to protection."

— Oxford English Dictionary

A national passport legitimizes and represents the arbitrary frontier of a particular nation. As property of the government that issues it, this license can be denied for virtually any reason. In essence, it is a control device, used by government to limit the movement of its citizens, and to regulate the entry and exit of "foreigners."

When you are issued a passport, you are actually giving something up — your inalienable right to "leave any country" and return again, confirmed by Article 13(2) in the *Universal Declaration of Human Rights*. In order to travel, you are forced to accept a bureaucratic device designed deliberately to control your movement. In legal terms, such a deceptive inducement to surrender a legal right is called fraud. Thus, if you have such a document, in a sense you have been robbed. To put it plainly, the national passport system is a swindle, the conscious theft of the individual's right to freedom of movement. In the world of nation-states, claims that citizens have freedom of travel are a hollow mockery. All states collude in perpetuating this fraud, beginning with their use of the word "passport" itself. The name of the document implies that it recognizes the right to travel when, in reality, it does the opposite. Although states are actually obliged to recognize this right, their passports do nothing less than impose limitations.

More appalling still, they make you pay for it. And in some places the fees are so high that the document is virtually unattainable. For citizens of affluent and allegedly "free" nations, the swindle only becomes apparent under extraordinary conditions. Some celebrity may be refused a passport on "political" grounds, for example, or someone may be persecuted while abroad. Finding themselves in legal or political trouble, travelers may have their passports revoked or confiscated. Suddenly, they are at the mercy of a "foreign" bureaucracy. In such circumstances, the traveller will quickly find that the lack of a "valid" passport is considered a "crime of omission." In response to this modern problem, a thriving black market in stolen passports has evolved.

Even if a passport can be obtained, however, the traveler still has problems. The next question is, where can you go with it? Mere possession of a passport, you see, is not a "carte blanche" for world travel. Before Rhodesia became Zimbabwe, its passports were recognized only by South Africa and Switzerland. Passports issued by Hong Kong, Albania and the Cook Islands are valid for travel to a severely limited number of sister states. Citizens of the United States should also take note: in many places your passport will not be enough. Before admitting U.S. passport holders, over 70 states around the world require visas. For non-citizens entering the U.S., of course, a visa is always mandatory. In "the land of the free," no foreign passport is accepted by itself.

City-dwellers seeking passports in African states are often favored over bush-dwellers. The rich, in Africa as elsewhere, are favored over the poor; they can afford the issuing fees and can pay their way home in the event of trouble abroad. This is a concern for both the traveller and the state. As actual "owner" of the passports it issues, the state assumes liability if some sister-state makes an accusation against a bearer who is considered "undesireable." The accused visitor may be arbitrarily detained, held in what the state calls "protective custody," and then returned to his native country at the expense of his government. Once home, the discredited traveler will more than likely face trial and conviction for having behaved badly abroad. When people leave their countries because of political or economic oppression, legal problems, or the threat of military service they often prefer prison abroad over being returned home. For those forced to flee, repatriation may mean death. In such cases, what good is their national passport? It's a liability if they keep it. It implies that the traveler, like the document itself, is the property of his or her government. Better to be "stateless" and without documents. For many refugees, in short, a national passport is not only a swindle; it can be a death trap.

Unsafe Passage

"The state is but a myth which perpetuates itself daily."
— Ernest Renan, 19th Century Philosopher

How did the passport swindle evolve in the first place? Beginning in the 16th century, "passport letters" were issued by many states to grant safe passage for people and property during wars. Often provided by neutral states in order for their vessels to move freely, the letters represented the right to safe passage. It was not until the mid-19th century that France and other European nation-states introduced documents that could be carried by any citizen who wished to travel. At this point, Great Britain and the United States still did not issue them — except during international conflicts. Although much of the planet was ruled by autocracies, it was, in contrast with the present, an unregulated world without mandatory passports, visas, quotas or work permits.

In the early 20th century passport documents became a simple convenience, issued at the request of the traveler. It was still possible, however, to travel overseas with nothing more than a boat ticket. After World War I, however, the passport controls instituted in the U.S. as wartime security measures were institutionalized and expanded. James Ramsey MacDonald, founder of the British Labor Party and Prime Minister from 1924 to 1935, is credited with launching the modern passport system. In 1925, it became a crime under British law to "forge" a passport or to lie in order to obtain one. Thus, a nation-state granted itself the exclusive right to issue travel documents. Since then, the system has spread around the world, gradually becoming obligatory.

Ironically, the first non-political or refugee passport predates the British grab for control. In the aftermath of the First World War and the Russian Revolution, Fridtjof Nansen, the Norwegian Arctic explorer, zoologist and statesman, came up with the idea. Nansen, who was Norway's delegate to the League of Nations, convinced his fellow delegates to establish an extra-territorial and anational passport for stateless persons and refugees, then mostly White Russians, who were living in Europe. For people deprived of "official" papers and those persecuted by national bureaucrats, it fulfilled a vital need. Without identification they could be detained in wretched camps for indefinite periods. The "Nansen Passport," issued to individuals of varying national origins, became the first truly international identification and travel document.

Nansen was awarded the Nobel Peace Prize in 1922 for his efforts. Over the succeeding 20 years the Nansen Office of Refugees (NOR), with a narrow mandate, meager funds, and official status conferred by the League, struggled heroically to cope with the growing problem of refugee identification. In 1938, the NOR itself received the Nobel Prize. But the League of Nations had disintegrated by this time. During World War II the NOR was replaced by the International Refugee Organization (IRO). With the founding of the United Nations in 1945, responsibility for refugees was passed on to the United Nations High Commissioner for Refugees (HCR) Office. In 1954, the HCR received the Nobel Peace Prize. But the Office was largely impotent, since control over identity and travel documents had been assumed by the nation-states.

By definition, the refugee is the most immediate victim of the anarchic relations between "sovereign" states. In recognizing that identification of refugees is an act of world peace, the Nobel judges have more than once implicitly condemned the "frontier world" of nation-states as a major barrier. Yet even the efforts of these honorable organizations have failed to win for stateless people the innate and inalienable rights guaranteed to everyone else.

Perpetual Harrassment

Today most citizens of developed countries travel for personal reasons. According to one survey of the Passport Office of the U.S. Department of State, almost 70 percent of the people who request passports say that their reasons for traveling are either "pleasure" or "personal." Only six percent have business reasons, about five percent are doing government work, and 2.5 percent are traveling abroad to study. Nevertheless, despite the fact that the overwhelming majority of people travel for clearly non-political purposes, they are obliged to carry an essentially political form of identification. If an American citizen wants to return home, in fact, he or she must either produce a "valid passport" or pay a $25 "service fee" to request that an exception be made.

The fee is not merely a form of extortion; it is unconstitutional. In *Aptheker v. Secretary of State*, the U.S. Supreme Court affirmed a constitutional right to travel closely related to rights of free speech and association. This right is linked to both the First and Fifth Amendment, and cannot be abridged even on political grounds. It follows, then, that imposing a financial penalty or refusing a person entry to his own country for lack of an "official" document violates the letter as well as the spirit of U.S. law.

There is, however, an ominous exception to this rule. The modern requirement that anyone who enters or leaves the United States must have a passport was codified in the Immigration and Nationality Act of 1952. Under this law, it is unlawful for citizens of the United States to enter or exit the country without a valid passport during a time of national emergency.

On January 17, 1953, a state of national emergency was declared by "lame duck" President Harry Truman. The Korean War was ending, but the Cold War had just begun. Three days later President Dwight Eisenhower was inaugurated. Nevertheless, Truman's last-minute proclamation established a state of permanent emergency, giving the Secretary of State authority to issue passports and limit their validity to travel in certain places. No democratic process was involved, yet a bureaucratic agency of the government was granted absolute power over the movement of all U.S. citizens. That "State of Emergency" has never been terminated.

Passport restrictions also infringe on the rights of a variety of international civil servants. For many such people, loyalty to a particular nation has been superceded by an international allegiance. For example, the Secretary-General of the United Nations and his staff, according to the UN Charter (art. 101), "shall not seek or receive instructions from any government or from any authority external to the Organization. They shall refrain from any action which might reflect on their position as international officials responsible only to the organization." Similar pledges are required from those employed by NATO, UNESCO, and numerous Non-Governmental Organizations (NGOs). Yet there is no international government to issue their passports. As a result, they must cope with national passports, supplemented by various identity cards that verify their status.

Even Red Cross officials find their work hampered by the lack of a neutral travel document. Problems often arise when a Red Cross worker's national passport is unfamiliar to a sister-state that may, paradoxically, need Red Cross aid. Only Swiss Red Cross officials consistently avoid such hassles; their passports carry a red cross on the cover.

Voyaging on the frontierless high seas, seamen also find national passports ludicrously restrictive. Forced to possess an exclusive territorial document while fulfilling an essentially non-territorial task, these "trans-national" citizens are frequently frustrated by expiration dates, visa requirements, and changes of government that can render national passports invalid. For sailors and those in related professions — transatlantic pilots, stewards and stewardesses, travel agents, as well as officers of multinational corporations, international journalists, artists, scientists, migrant workers and anyone else engaged in work of an apolitical and transnational character, the national passport system is not only a colossal nuisance. Allowing perpetual bureaucratic harrassment, it offends human dignity. Like refugees and anyone else who has ever faced a bored and arrogant frontier guard, "trans-national" workers recognize it as a fraud which, given any choice, they would not endure.

Above and Beyond

If you need any further evidence of the national passport swindle, you need only look up. Since the 1960s, astronauts, cosmonauts and shuttle crews have orbited above our heads, giving testimony through their movements to the self-evident oneness of the planet and the myopia demonstrated by efforts to keep it divided. These travelers literally and dramatically represent the sovereignty of the human race. It may seem foolish to ask, but do shuttle crews need national passports when they leave Earth? Are they asked to present "valid" documents upon re-entry? Obviously not. They pass no national frontier upon take-off, and break no law when, without a passport, they return. They travel as humans, not merely as national citizens. They are, in fact, truly world citizens. Through their journeys they become pioneers of our common destiny. Traveling through space they break a barrier more profound than sound; they push past the barrier of nationalism and help make world citizenship a reality.

The human venture into space has raised our civic status to the planetary level. Finally, we must face the reality that this planet is our common home. Despite all the nationalistic prayers, the Almighty did not create sub-divisions called nations. Neither does He sanction or bless them. He created only a world community, indivisible by definition. Looking at the world from the perspective of the heavens, all passports appear at the very least superfluous.

Chapter 17

The World Passport: Tool & Symbol

The first World Passport was a relatively modest document, a 16-page green-covered information and identification booklet with space for visas. The text was in English and Esperanto. On May 10, 1954, a thousand were printed, with copies sent to the United Nations and the U.S. Department of Justice. Samples were also mailed to ambassadors based in Washington, officials of the 79 existing national governments of the world, and leading travel agency federations.

By the end of the summer, responses began to arrive. Most governments, though acknowledging receipt of the documents, remained non-committal. Ecuador, Laos and Yemen, however, agreed to recognize the passport on a de facto (case-by-case) basis.

My early attempts to use the document myself proved frustrating. But finally, with the help of my World Guard uniform and a curious reporter from the *Times of India* at Bombay airport, I managed to enter India. Returning to the West in 1957 also proved complicated. Ultimately, however, U.S. Immigration officials stood aside. They had decided, for the moment, to avoid confrontation over an issue that seemed to transcend their authority. (See *My Country Is The World*, Juniper Ledge Publishing Co, D.C., 1985).

The second edition of the passport came off the press in 1972. Now it was in five languages and had 36 pages, with space for a full medical history — a first for any passport. The initial run of 2,000 was quickly exhausted. It was slowly becoming a useful tool for a wide variety of people. For North Africans, Turks, and

Asian refugees it represented the hope of a permanent residence in Europe. For the countercultural young it was the "Earth Passport." In addition, a number of businessmen found it useful as a "back up" document that might insure them from the political liability of their own national citizenship.

At this point, the movement's home base was in France, where I had been living since 1960. In September, 1972, about six months after the new World Passport began to circulate, the French government attacked. I was charged with "swindling," selling swindled goods (recel) and "confusing the public mind."

Subsequent legal maneuvers took almost two years. By the time it was over, we had moved the offices of the World Service Authority (WSA), which issued the documents, to the French-Swiss frontier town, Basel, and incorporated as a non-profit association under Swiss law. Despite losing in French court, we continued issuing documents from Basel. Ecuador, Zambia, Upper Volta (Burkina Faso) and Mauritania gave the passport de jure (official and legal) recognition, and demand continued to increase.

The third edition — in seven languages, including Russian, Arabic and Esperanto — was designed in 1975. It had evolved considerably since my first attempt almost 20 years earlier. Now the World Passport had 42 pages, including a six page section for affiliate identifications.

For the increasing number of people without "valid" identity documents, the WSA passport presented a unique advantage: the right to leave any country, including one's own. It also placed responsibility squarely on the individual who used it, rather than giving the burden of liability (or the power of control over movement) to the state. As World Citizens, holders of the World Passport understood that their right to travel, outlined in the document, was grounded in the *Universal Declaration of Human Rights* and the *Charter of the United Nations*. The passport itself was simply a symbol of that right. Passports went out and stories came in: Families were being separated because the husband and wife, with passports from different countries, were expelled from their homes for political reasons. People seeking specialized treatment outside their own countries were either unable to obtain travel documents, or found that their documents weren't accepted abroad. Others were being held in arbitrary detention merely because their travel or identity documents weren't accepted as valid. For such reasons and many others, the list of World Citizens grew.

We heard from hapless travelers whose passports were lost or stolen. We corresponded with unfortunate victims of domestic instability, stranded because their government was replaced by a more hostile regime while they were away. We learned about the illogic of inter-governmental policies that sometimes made it impossible to complete a journey. And we collected graphic evidence that a form of neutral identification was sorely needed by the many people whose efforts are humanitarian or international in nature.

Since 1975, more than 300,000 passports have been issued through World Service Authority offices in Europe, Japan and the United States. World Passports are currently recognized on an unofficial basis by more than 100 nations that have issued visas based on the document or allowed holders to enter. Available to any human being, the passport is a 40-page document, with text in seven languages — English, French, Spanish, Arabic, Russian, Chinese and Esperanto. Inside the hard cardboard cover, it contains 27 visa pages with six pages for affiliate identifications. On the inside back cover is a three-fold complete medical certificate with spaces for blood type, vaccinations and a personal medical history.

Some people have urgent uses for the document. For others it is a convenience, a "second" passport that provides peace of mind. As any traveler who has experienced an automobile accident abroad knows, the first thing the police take is your passport. Hotels often want to hold your passport. Even if you don't plan to leave a country suddenly, having a spare passport helps, whether the issue is cashing travelers checks or simply proving who you are.

Obviously there are no guarantees. But this is true for any travel document. Warnings aside, the fact of the matter is that wide-ranging travel with a World Passport is possible. Thousands of people around the world use them.

Identifying its holder as a sovereign being with the right to travel, the WSA passport represents that right in a form that no nation can ignore. As more people use these and other World

Citizen documents, more national governments are obliged to accept them. In some cases, accepting the World Passport of a refugee may become a matter of principle. Most of the time, however, nations faced with stateless people simply bow to necessity.

In either case, it works!

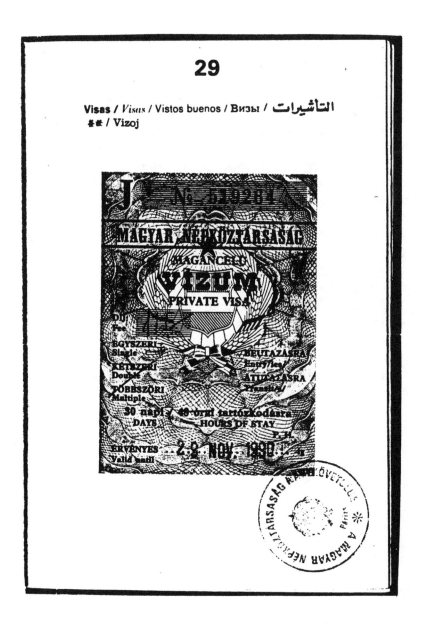

Chapter 18

Credo of a World Citizen

A World Citizen is a human being who lives intellectually, morally and physically in the present. A World Citizen accepts the dynamic fact that the planetary human community is interdependent and whole, that humankind is essentially one.

A World Citizen is a peaceful and peacemaking individual, both in daily life and in contacts with others.

As a global person, a World Citizen relates directly to humankind and to all fellow humans spontaneously, generously and openly. Mutual trust is basic to his/her life style.

Politically, a World Citizen accepts a sanctioning institution of representative government, expressing the general and individual sovereign will in order to establish and maintain a system of just and equitable world law with appropriate legislative, judicial and enforcement bodies.

A World Citizen brings about better understanding and protection of different cultures, ethnic groups and language communities by promoting the use of a neutral international language, such as Esperanto. A World Citizen makes this world a better place to live in harmoniously by studying and respecting the viewpoints of fellow citizens anywhere in the world.

Chapter 19

World Citizenship — the Basics

As I've mentioned already, when you put "world" in front of "citizen" you have jumped from the framework of the nation-state to the global level. In doing so, you have re-empowered yourself as a human being.

But there is more: In declaring yourself a World Citizen, you have joined a global system. You have redefined yourself and made a new social contract with other members of a global community. As a sovereign individual, you have chosen a higher allegiance — to humanity rather than to an exclusive group called a nation. Who gives you the authority to take this step? No one. You simply take it. Why can you do that? Because citizens — not governments — are the true source of sovereignty. This basic truth is enshrined in the founding documents of most nations, as well as in the *Universal Declaration of Human Rights*. You have a right to the social and political system of your choice — without strings attached. You have a human right to dignity and freedom, a right to express your opinions, to assemble, and to associate. You have a right to leave and enter the place you call home.

In becoming a World Citizen, you are saying: "Thank you for defining my rights. Now I'm claiming them. From now on, my country is the world." And to do it, you only have to prove one thing: that you're a human being.

***

After reading this far, you probably have some questions and concerns. They may be philosophical or just practical. You may be wondering, for instance: Is all this really necessary? Is it possible, or even safe? What, after all, is World Citizenship really about?

Let's start from the beginning.

Why should anyone become a World Citizen? Is it really necessary?

If we are ever going to solve the truly "global" problems we face — war, poverty and ecological degradation — we certainly need a better system than a current collection of mutually exclusive nations. To achieve civic peace in our interdependent world, a new and all-encompassing social contract will be essential. Somehow we must express our common humanity. This is a process, one that begins with the recognition of our innate and inalienable world citizenship.

Isn't "International Law" enough?

Laws don't magically appear. A legislative body must enact the laws, and, if they are going to mean anything, some executive authority must administer them. To ensure justice, there must also be a judicial body, and some way to enforce its decisions. If the laws are just, enforcement will be minimal. Essentially, law requires some kind of government. But the existing mish-mash of international laws lacks this supporting structure. "International law" is merely a matrix of multinational treaties between independent, sovereign states. Neither the individual nor humanity itself is or can be fairly represented.

Does humanity have rights?

Certainly. As you know, if humanity itself dies, each individual dies. And we also know that the individual has a right to live. Therefore, humanity has this right. In the past, we might have considered the relationship between the individual and the whole theoretical. In the nuclear age, however, it has become practical and dynamic.

What about the right to choose my political allegiance?

The right of self-determination is defined in the *United Nations Charter*, as well as in the *International Covenant on Human Rights*. The *Universal Declaration of Human Rights*, in Articles 15(2) and 21(3), sanctions the legal expression of individual will as the basis of government. In national law, many constitutions refer specifically to fundamental human rights. The U.S. Constitution defines human rights as inalienable, and U.S. case law has acknowledged the Universal Declaration as "common binding international law." (Ref: Filartiga v. Pena-Irala, 876 2d 1980)

What's the relationship between world and national citizenship?

National citizenship is exclusive. World citizenship is inclusive. In a sense, then, they are mutually exclusive. But the concept of "citizenship" can also be visualized as a series of concentric circles, the first or inner one local and the outermost global. This approach to citizenship incorporates both the individual and general good.

Must I renounce my national citizenship in order to be a world citizen?

Unless you want to make a clean break for some personal reason, you needn't bother. Look at it this way: Exclusive nationality doesn't protect and represent you in terms of global problems such as war. In a sense, it has renounced you already. In declaring yourself a world citizen, you "renounce" nothing, but instead "transcend" your limited national identity. Major world "revolutions" of the 20th Century have rendered the 18th Century political idea of national citizenship obsolete. You are simply keeping pace with reality.

But don't I lose my nationality if I do it?

No. Since the individual is fundamentally sovereign, you have the right to choose your own political allegiance. Your nationality has two aspects — cultural (or ethnic) and political. The laws regarding political allegiance neither deny nor prohibit your adding world citizenship to your lesser citizenships. In any case, society itself is not exclusively national. It is both local (or municipal) and global at the same time.

How many World Citizens are there?

Approximately one million people have registered since the movement began in Paris in 1948. About 350,000 of them have World Passports.

Practically speaking, how do I claim to be a World Citizen?

You register with the World Service Authority, an administrative agency established in 1954 to promote world peace and develop world government. Once you pay the registration fee, you receive a World Citizen Card, a wallet-sized, numbered and laminated document, printed in seven languages. The card confirms that you are a registered citizen of the World Government of World Citizens. In addition, you receive a form letter — also in seven languages — that you can send to the head of your national government, informing him or her of your new status. In legal terms, this is known as "constructive notice."

Wait a minute! What World Government?

It stands to reason, doesn't it? Citizens need some form of government to serve them and express their social contract. In this case, it was founded on September 4, 1953 in Ellsworth, Maine in order to protect the rights of World Citizens against violations by national officials. Its mandates are the *Universal Declaration of Human Rights* and the *Stockholm Declaration* of 1972, which includes ecological rights. The World Service Authority, a District of Columbia Corporation, acts as its administrative arm.

In addition, this embryonic government has commissions to develop solutions in areas such as communication, education, economics, health, and science. In 1972, a provisional World Court of Human Rights was founded. More recently, a World Citizens political party was established to provide an electoral vehicle for those interested in promoting the global agenda of world citizenship in their communities. World Government does not yet have a constitution, nor does it really require one in order to begin the implementation of a new civic agreement. Governments start when people acknowledge allegiance. That, of course, has already happened. But the long-term political program of World Government does include the development and drafting of a constitution, as well as a convention attended by delegates elected from among the registered citizens, and ultimately, the ratification of this world constitution by the public.

It will take time, of course, perhaps as long as ten years. At the moment, however, World Government already has more citizens than the following 24 members of the United Nations:

Bahrain	412,000
Barbados	250,000
Belize	160,000
Brunei	220,000
Cape Verde	300,000
Comoros	460,000
Cyprus	675,000
Djibouti	360,000
Dominica	74,000
Equatorial Guinea	280,000
Fiji	695,000
Gambia	715,000
Grenada	114,000
Iceland	240,000
Luxembourg	365,000
Maldives	175,000
Malta	360,000
St. Christopher	45,000
St. Lucia	120,000
Seychelles	66,000
Solomon Islands	270,000
Suriname	375,000
Swaziland	660,000
Vanuatu	130,000
Western Samoa	160,000

Are the documents issued by the World Service Authority valid?

Any government has the right to issue documents. Acting on behalf of World Government, the WSA provides registered citizens with identity cards, birth and marriage certificates, press credentials, international exit visas, international resident permits and World Passports. In particular, the authority to issue passports stems from the inalienable right of human beings to travel freely, a right partially identified in Article 13(2) of the Human Rights Declaration. The proof of this authority lies in the fact that more than 100 nations accept World Passports. Several nations have made this acceptance official.

What if a World Citizen is a criminal or breaks the law while abroad?

On the surface this sounds like a valid concern. We may not know that we have issued a passport to a dangerous person. But that same criminal could enter a hardware store and purchase a knife. Should the hardware store owner know the identity of every customer, and what he or she plans to do with a potential weapon? The seller of a document is no more responsible for what a buyer does with it than the seller of a knife or a postage stamp. When you buy a stamp from the post office, you can send a love letter or a bomb. The person providing the stamps is in no way responsible for what you put inside your package. The relationship between the World Service Authority and World Citizens is exactly the same; it simply provides a service.

But what if the person uses a WSA document to commit a crime?

When this occurs, we usually receive a call from law enforcement officials asking for information. Since the person involved has abused his or her privilege, we open our files. But we are not in control of that individual's behavior, and we are not responsible. In fact, everyone who receives a document from the World Service Authority is also notified that WSA is not responsible for its use.

On the other hand, if you use a document appropriately and run into trouble, World Government is there to help.

Chapter 20

Proof of Rights

A t first the only document available to World Citizens was an identity card. In 1954, a passport was added, and an administrative office was established to process the many requests for information and help that began to arrive. As years have passed, new situations have required creative thinking — and additional tools to deal with the problems posed by the rigidity of national bureaucracies. Although the logic of basic human rights is crystal clear, it has nevertheless led the World Service Authority in some unusual directions. Nation-states continue to insist on setting up barriers that make it difficult for some people to marry or even leave a country. Such obstacles call for bold action. As a result, other forms of documentation have been designed.

World Marriage Certificate

In every human society, marriage is the most important legal contract, combining the continuity of the species with the elements of passion, economic cooperation, and cohabitation. Although linked in the past to primitive concepts of property and male dominance, it is commonly viewed today as a voluntary agreement between consenting adults, and defined as such in Article 16 of the *Universal Declaration of Human Rights*.

The Declaration does not place any restrictions on the right to marry. A couple needn't be the same nationality, color, race, or religion. Many nation-states, however, dispute this fundamental right. In Israel, for instance, you must be Jewish in order to obtain a marriage certificate. And if you are a foreigner who wants to marry in Germany, you must produce a certificate from your home country indicating that there are no impediments.

For Yusuf Kaya, the Turkish World Citizen who fell in love with a Romanian refugee, this posed a considerable problem when the two decided to wed. Although Kaya had managed, with the help of a lawyer and World Government documents, to win residency in Germany, the state refused to issue a marriage license. The lovers appealed to the World Service Authority for aid. Our response was to issue them a World Marriage Certificate.

Why should any nation, we reasoned, have the power to prohibit a couple who love each other and consent to share their lives from marrying? Government should merely confirm the decision made by the individuals rather than judging it and imposing conditions. The World Marriage Certificate, combining the mandate of the Human Rights Declaration with the method of the Quakers, allows couples to marry themselves. All that World Government does is verify this voluntary agreement.

World Political Asylum Card

In many places, asylum is a vital and often controversial question. Although the general concept refers to shelter for the unfortunate, political asylum normally involves one state's willingness to shelter the citizen of another state from persecution. It is commonly perceived as a horizontal relationship between nation-states, resulting in a grant to the inidividual.

In reality, however, asylum is a human right, a claim to freedom from persecution that can be made by any individual. But how can you make that claim valid? Despite the fact that freedom from persecution is guaranteed by the Human Rights Declaration, people are turned away every day. Faced with Salvadorans fleeing Death Squads, U.S. Immigration officials refuse and attempt to send them home. Boat people in Hong Kong and Chinese expatriates in Japan face the same problem. Under such circumstances, there is only one choice left: to claim asylum on another level. Prevented from moving horizontally, you can move vertically and claim world political asylum. After all, that is precisely what the Human Rights Declaration implies.

In order to do this, though, you must first declare yourself as a World Citizen. You must move beyond the level of nation-states. This isn't much different than saying you aren't a New Yorker or a Bavarian but rather an American or a German. Having claimed your status as a World Citizen, you can automatically claim asylum. The card provided by the World Service Authority, along with the back up of the office, defines your rights. In several languages, it explains that, under Article 14 of the Declaration, "Everyone has the right to seek and enjoy . . . asylum from persecution."

When confronted by a national bureaucrat who says, "You can't stay here," the World Citizen appeals to a higher law. National laws regarding asylum can be complex and vary from one country to the next. But national officials are quite hesitant to deny asylum when the claim is buttressed by international law and clear documentation.

International Exit Visa

Some countries, including the United States, allow visitors and citizens to exit freely. But in other cases, even if you have a passport and a visa, you may find it difficult to leave. Even though the Human Rights Declaration says that you have this right, violations are common.

To neutralize such a problem, you may need another type of visa. But the nation that is holding you up is not likely to provide it. The alternative is again to operate on a higher — "meta"— level. All UN member nations recognize, at least on paper, that people have the right to leave any country. It has thus become an international right. Based on this fact, the World Service Authority issues international exit visas for holders of World Passports. Placed on the first visa page of your passport, it defines your "right to leave." The border bureaucrat who reviews this document may be confused or even embarrassed. But confronted with international law and a well-prepared World Citizen, he is not likely to stand in your way.

International Resident Permit

A little known but revolutionary fact is the right of residency . . . anywhere! Allied with freedom of movement, the right of residence is cited in Article 13(1) of the *Universal Declaration of Human Rights:* "Everyone has the right of freedom of movement and residence within the borders of each state." What the framers had in mind is not entirely clear, but interpreted literally it means exactly what it says: anyone can live anywhere. Based on that right, the World Service Authority issues an "International Resident Permit" to registered World Citizens. It is inserted in their World Passports on an empty visa page. In March, 1990, all national governments were informed about the issuance of both the International Exit Visa and the International Resident Permit.

***

These documents and the others that have evolved out of the experiences of various World Citizens over the years are not designed simply to perplex bureaucrats — though very often they do deserve it. Each one, beginning with the World Passport itself, addresses a specific aspect of the basic human right to travel and live where we please.

Some people will argue that this is impossible or even dangerous. "You can't open the frontiers," they will say. "People will simply flood in." That reasoning reflects an approach to human relations known as "lifeboat ethics." When someone says that the developed countries — the world of the "haves" — cannot open their frontiers to the "have-nots" of Vietnam or El Salvador, the real message is: we have it and we plan to keep it.

That admission, in turn, opens up a variety of economic and political questions. Can we continue to allow the world to be unfairly divided — one quarter "have" and three quarters "have not"? Can we possibly justify the deaths of 40,000 children a day through starvation while spending billions of dollars every day on weapons? As much as eight percent of the world's gross product is wasted on armaments, and every bullet manufactured is taking bread out of someone's mouth. While a small, privileged minority lives in relative comfort, poverty, homelessness and hunger increase. How much longer can we hide behind our borders and refuse to view the problem in holistic terms? For a stranded traveler or a desperate refugee, a World Passport or an International Exit Visa may be a life-saving tool. For a political activist, it may function simply as a symbol. In truth, these documents are both — and more. They put into practice a new social contract that encompasses the sovereignty of every person and the unity of humanity as a whole.

Chapter 21

Using Your Passport

Few people are more exploited and despised in the passport swindle of the nation-state than the lowly frontier bureaucrat. Assigned to stand guard at the farthest edge of his nation's territory, he is both victim and oppressor. His job is "to control;" his approach is to consider everyone who passes before him "guilty" until innocence is proven through the presentation of some piece of paper. The paper is "valid" if he or some superior says so.

Perhaps only one occupation is more morally and intellectually debilitating — diplomat. A diplomat's surroundings may be more elegant, and his pay is certainly better. But he has a similar ritualistic function, performed with his nation's armed forces at his back. Though situated at very different points along the totem-pole of national sovereignty, the frontier guard and the diplomat are both basically degraded servants whose work requires the sacrifice of their humanity.

Night and day, the frontier guard remains at his post, examining people as they attempt to pass inspection. Such undignified work usually leads to boredom and an anger that manifests itself in confused arrogance. Protecting the nation is the last thing on a frontier guard's mind.

Then one day, without warning, you walk up and present a World Passport. What should you do? And what must you expect?

Gaining Acceptance

When you present yourself and your documents with confidence, you have at least a 50 percent chance of approval on your first attempt. Keep in mind that more than 100 nations have accepted World Passports and other documents over the past few decades. A current list of nations that grant de facto and de jure approval is available from the World Service Authority.

Your basic goal is to "decontrol" the guard with your manner and papers. Since the world currently consists of 172 separate nation-states, with varying laws and customs, reaching that goal will require some ability to adapt. Keep in mind that you will be dealing initially with the "low man," someone who knows little about human rights or international law. Use the methods described earlier for "overruling bureaucracies" (pages 30–41). In particular:

- Get Organized
- Stay Cool
- Assume You are Right
- Use the Right Words
- Make Yourself Look Good, and
- Remain Firm

In addition, the following tips may help when presenting your passport or other documents to a national bureaucrat:

1. Whenever you speak with an official, have a copy of the *Universal Declaration of Human Rights* in your possession. Be prepared to quote Articles 13(2), 15(2), 28 and 30. These are essential mandates for the utilization of your document, especially the World Passport.

Article 13(2)

Everyone has the right to leave any country, including his own, and to return to his country.

Article 15(2)

No one shall be arbitrarily deprived of his nationality nor denied the right to change his nationality.

Article 28

Everyone is entitled to a social and international order in which the freedoms set forth in this Declaration can be fully realized.

Article 30

Nothing in this Declaration may be interpreted as implying any State, group or person has any right to engage in any act aimed at the destruction of any of the rights and freedoms set forth herein.

2. You should also have excerpts from the United Nations Charter on hand, and be ready to cite the relevant reference to human rights. If necessary, mention Articles 55 and 56, which refer to member-states agreement to respect and observe fundamental human rights. Keep in mind that these rights refer to YOU.

Article 55

With a view to the creation of conditions of stability and well-being which are necessary for peaceful and friendly relations among nations based on respect for the principle of equal rights and self-determination of peoples, the United Nations shall promote . . . universal respect for, and observance of, human rights and fundamental freedoms for all without distinction as to race, sex, language and religion.

Article 56

All members pledge . . . to take joint and separate action in cooperation with the Organization for the achievement of the purposes set forth in Article 55.

3. When you are interviewed, keep the questionnaire form of the World Judicial Commission in plain view. Before you begin, fill in the appropriate blanks: name, date, country, location, passport number, date of issue, and so on. If the official asks about it, explain that as a registered World Citizen you are obliged to report all violations of fundamental human rights to the World Judicial Commission in Champaign, Illinois.

Keep in mind that consular officers operate from specific instructions and guidelines established by their ministries. They cannot arbitrarily deviate from these. Therefore, you have a right to request the basis of their authority for any action, including refusal of a visa or rejection of your passport. If they can cite no specific directive, remind them that they have no legal reason to refuse. The principle here is: what is neither denied nor prohibited is permitted. The questionnaire makes it clear that you plan to follow up.

4. If necessary, display a copy of the *WSA Sample Visa Booklet*, sample visas on WSA Passports. This reference will confirm the legitimacy of your document. You may also show copies of official letters of *de juris* recognition from several national governments.

5. Attempt to secure visas from countries that allow easier access. Doing this does not oblige you to visit these countries. When you have visas from any nation, your request to a less accessible nation gains credibility. **Remember: the credibility of a passport derives not from its issuing authority but from its acceptance by another country.**

6. Report any inappropriate treatment. Officials of national government must deal with you in a neutral manner, giving objective consideration to your request. If they do not, the World Judicial Commission and World Service Authority can provide recourse—but only if you provide complete information.

7. Don't lose sight of the basic truth: you have a right to travel, and the frontier is nothing but a symbolic barrier. Your passport validates your right to cross it. The most insidious force working against you is a sense of guilt. Believing that the frontier is "real," you think that you must prove you are "innocent" enough to pass through. That guilty feeling is a result of a lifetime of conditioning by the nation-state system. It can make you wait at a border station when there is no one around, or even stand in the driving rain while a bureaucrat remains inside. Whatever you do, don't act like a guilty fugitive. If you truly want the freedom to travel, you have to begin by realizing that you already have it.

Transcending Rejection

Your initial objective, in an interview at the frontier, is to evoke a response. Once the official engages in dialogue on your terms, half the battle has been won. Nevertheless, you may be turned away at first. In such instances, there is no need to be discouraged. A negative response is not necessarily final. Refusal can actually mark the beginning of a fruitful and ultimately successful exchange. "The sale begins when the client says no." Your documents are powerful tools with which you can argue your point and, perhaps, educate the bureaucrat. In any case, keep one thing in mind: you are right and the bureaucrat is wrong.

If you have used all the material and arguments at your disposal and still find yourself on the wrong side of a particular frontier, at least three options still remain.

1. Leave.

No, this doesn't mean "give up" and go to some other country. Just wait awhile, in a coffee shop or international area, out of the inflexible official's view. The frontier is always no man's land — the space between nations. It belongs to US.

When you attempt to enter almost any country, time is on your side. If you are rejected at first, a one or two hour wait will usually be enough. By the time you return, the bureaucrat who rejected you will probably be gone. The chances that he mentioned your particular case to his replacement are slim indeed.

Refreshed and rehearsed, try again with a new person. Since the business of travel is ultimately arbitrary, the chances that you will be allowed to enter increase with each attempt. Each nation has its own standards regarding who should enter or leave. With so many people travelling and so many different types of passports, it is impossible for the guard at the frontier to recognize each one or judge its validity with any sort of certainty.

In law there is a saying, "If it quacks like a duck, it is a duck." Similarly, many border guards simply assume: if it looks like a passport, it probably is.

2. Ask for Higher Authority.

When things get rough, however, you need to remember who you are dealing with: a low-level bureaucrat, isolated at the bottom of a huge chain of command. He is no patriot, and he doesn't want trouble. Neither is he likely to be well-versed in matters of international law. If he gives you trouble, your objective, then, is to place him on the defensive by using the main human rights arguments at your disposal. During this exchange, politely ask for his name, rank and number. If he grumbles, you need only explain, as matter-of-factly as possible, that he is forcing you to go over his head. Since you are not part of his chain of command, you can explain that you may have to "go to the top."

First, ask to see his superior. You may find that, at the next level in the hierarchy, the desire to avoid controversy will neutralize the doubts about the "validity" of your document. At this level, your supporting documents will also carry more weight, particularly if other World Citizens have been admitted to the country in the past. Be polite, but firm. Remind the official of his duty to respect international law.

Empathy may also be a useful tool. Like most police and jailers, border officials feel unappreciated. They want to be liked, even loved. Their work provides little opportunity to meet these basic needs. By empathizing with their situation, you may win on the emotional level what you have been unable to achieve through reason.

On the other hand, you may not. In that case:

3. Threaten to Expose Them.

Anger rarely serves you well. The most effective tone is a quiet but adamant assurance. Simply spell out what you must do: report this violation of human rights. You can mention high ministries of the government involved , but don't neglect to add your intention to seek redress in the world judicial community.

For exactly such purposes, a World Court of Human Rights was established in 1972. It embodies a "world bill of rights," defining guarantees relating to deprivation of life, inhumane treatment, slavery and forced labor, personal liberty, determination of rights, procedural safeguards in criminal cases, as well as freedom of conscience, expression, peaceable assembly and movement. In the absence of a world constitution, the functions of the Court are performed by the World Judicial Commission, to which human rights violations against any World Citizen can be reported.

In addition to the *Declaration of Human Rights* and UN Charter, you may want to make reference to relevant UN Resolutions and the *International Covenants on Economic, Social and Cultural Rights* and *Civil and Political Rights*. One of the bases of World Citizenship, for example, is the principle of self-determination, codifed by these documents. Self-determination recognizes the individual's right to choose his or her political status. As a World Citizen, you have chosen World Government and become part of a new "people." According to UN Resolution 2625:

> "The establishment of a sovereign and independent state, the free association within an independent state or the emergence into any other political status freely determined by a people constitute modes of implementing the right of self-determination of that people."

In other words, World Citizens are a self-determining people, who have pledged their allegiance to a declared government of their choice. This government functions independently and outside the nation-state framework.

If, despite all your arguments, you are denied entry into a country, remind the border bureaucrats that a variety of consequences will follow:

- High officials of their government will be forced to respond, since you have no intention of letting the matter slide. This will include both your actions and the intervention of the World Service Authority.
- The bureaucrat who made the decision on your document will be forced to defend it, based on specific statutes as well as international law. Remember: international law is on YOUR side.
- Unfavorable publicity will follow. Make it clear that you plan to inform the international press. If possible, plan ahead and have the press meet you at the entry point. The presence of journalists and cameras may be enough to tip the decision in your favor.

Any bureaucrat who doesn't flinch by this time is either better informed than you might think or incredibly ignorant. Either way, you are at the end of the line. Having exhausted all appeals to reason and emotion, only two choices are left: walk away or make a scene.

Even if you walk away, you haven't failed. You have simply postponed the matter until another day. Some other World Citizen will probably carry on the struggle. To help, however, you should report the encounter in as much detail as possible to the World Service Authority, which can file a protest on your behalf. Through correspondence, the WSA may be able to reverse the initial decision.

On the other hand, if you decide to resist the refusal, you are taking the problem to a new and more dramatic level. Your initial rejection is about to become an "international incident." This is a more challenging and difficult road to take, and certainly is not recommended if you have a deadline to meet. You may.be detained, removed by force, or even jailed for demanding your human rights. Whatever you do, keep your actions non-violent. Refuse to move, raise your voice, embarrass your captors if that serves your purposes. But never give them the opportunity to turn the confrontation into a fist-fight. The nation-state thrives on violence; your power, in contrast, stems from the righteousness of your creative and nonviolent defense of your basic human rights.

You may not be able to cross every frontier. But if you remain faithful to the principles of World Citizenship, you cannot lose.

Chapter 22

Travel Log, 1977–1984

In my current World Passport are the visas of seven nations, the entry stamps of European countries such as Bulgaria, Czechoslovakia and Romania, as well as those of Mexico, Haiti, Peru, Cyprus, New Zealand, and Singapore. Traveling as a World Citizen over the years I've seen India and the Middle East, helped Chinese students seeking refuge in Japan, witnessed historic changes sweep Eastern Europe, and confounded bureaucrats around the world.

Since declaring myself a World Citizen in 1948, in other words, I've personally field-tested much of the advice in this guidebook. As the ranks of World Government have grown, I've also been able to collect and assess numerous stories from other global pioneers. World Citizens have used their documents in escaping repressive regimes, establishing residency rights, and touring remote regions. Collectively, our experiences not only attest to the power of the WSA Passport as a symbol of one world, but also demonstrate its practical value.

On the other hand, it hasn't always been easy. For many nations, world citizenship has been a confusing nuisance; for a few it has become a threat that they insist on classifying as a crime. Such was the logic that led a French court to convict me of "counterfeiting" in 1977, based on my work with the World Service Authority, and to issue a bench warrant for my arrest. But by that time, I was in Israel. After entering on my "stateless" travel document in January, I had proceded to Jerusalem and declared the holy sites of the Jewish, Muslim, and Christian religions "world territory under the sovereign protection of world law."

Being allowed into the Holy Land, however, did not mean that Israel or its neighbors recognized my passport or World Government. That became unpleasantly clear when I tried to cross the Allenby Bridge into Jordan. Suddenly, I was caught on the line that separated the two countries. Israeli soldiers waited behind me on one side of the bridge, Jordanians faced me on the other. Ironically, their guns pointed at me, the only "peacenik" available. Eventually, word came down from Jerusalem: I was to be forced back into Israel until I could be returned to England. The Jordanians gratefully colluded, a bus being provided by them to "escort" me off the neutral line.

Once back in London, I embarked for the United States, and entered in late January with a U.S. tourist visa I had obtained from the U.S. consulate in Strasbourg. Reaching my Washington, D.C. office, I found it humming with activity. Applications were arriving from both U.S. citizens and resident aliens who recognized the value of a neutral, global travel document.

That Spring I returned again to London on business, and even visited Switzerland without incident. Two years before I had been jailed by the Swiss for "illegal entry." This time, though, I was pleased to meet with absolutely no resistance. Satisfied that everything was moving along perfectly, I returned to London and then flew to the United States for the second time since the start of the year.

Over the 29 years since renouncing my citizenship, I had often been allowed to enter the country by perplexed and frustrated U.S. Immigration officials. World Citizenship had been my only identity when returning home in 1953 and 1957. After living in Europe throughout the 1960s, visa requirements had nevertheless been waived when I landed at Kennedy Airport in June, 1975. The following year U.S. officials had examined my World Passport and again let me in without a peep. In May, 1977, however, the Immigration inspector at Dulles Airport was not impressed. Paging through the passport, which listed my birthplace as Maine and my residence as Washington, D.C., she decided that something was missing — a visa.

"I don't need one," I explained. "I live in Washington, and I'm just returning home. Actually, my passport is based on Article 13(2) of the Universal Declaration of Human Rights."

Her eyes turned cold. My explanation was apparently not reassuring. To this fearful bureaucrat I was either a lunatic or a potential terrorist. And our surroundings didn't help. I had deliberately waited for nearly two hours after landing before appearing in the international section. As a result, we were alone in the giant hall.

"Just a moment," she said. Inching away, she disappeared into a tiny office with my passport. Moments later, her frowning chief emerged, holding it gingerly in his hand as if it were hot.

The official eyed me cautiously, and then explained slowly, "We don't recognize this passport. If you aren't a U.S. citizen and possess no valid visa, we have to exclude you."

"But I live here," I protested. "I'm the president of a District of Columbia Corporation. I have an apartment on S Street."

"Sorry," he replied, handing my passport back, "but for Immigration you are an excludable alien. Would you like to make a statement? I can notarize it. That makes it legal."

It was the offer I had been waiting for. For the first time since 1948, I thought, here is an opportunity to engage the U.S. legal system. My case might even make it to the Supreme Court. But in order to go that far, I knew, a constitutional issue was essential. I chose the Ninth Amendment. According to Justice Douglas, it was the "sleeping giant" of U.S. constitutional law

***

For two days I was kept under guard by Pam-Am rent-a-cops at a Ramada Inn near the airport, and finally brought before an Immigration judge. The Ninth Amendment, I argued, affirms "inalienable" rights, one of which is the right to create a government where none already exists. By exercising not only a legitimate but a fundamental human right, I was issuing a wake-up call. The U.S. Constitution itself, I explained, implies the right to establish government — in my case, a World Government — and to issue passports and other documents from that government.

The judge was unconvinced, and upheld the initial classification: "excludable alien."

Although I was soon released, the threat of "deportation" now hung over my head. Nine months later, an Immigration Appeals Court upheld the earlier decision. As far as the U.S. government was concerned, I was living in the country allegally.

But where could I go? The moon was not a viable option. Nor were the oceans, even though they cover 70 percent of the planet's surface. I was subject to deportation, yet I was practically "undeportable." Sensing that it was the government and not myself who was backed against a wall, I decided to fight back. Maybe I was "allegal" in the eyes of a judge, but that apparently didn't prevent me from going to court. Relishing the contradiction, on July 17, 1979 I filed a lawsuit against the District Inspector of the INS in the 1st Federal District Court. My goal: a writ of habeas corpus enabling me to "enter" the United States legally.

Once again the court refused. The Justice Department simply argued that a "stateless" person with no valid visa had no right to enter the country. The court's decision — immediate deportation.

The state's action — nothing. I appealed.

The following May the U.S. Court of Appeals upheld the decision of the lower court, opening the door to my real goal: taking my case to the Supreme Court. Finally, I would argue the full implications of the U.S. Constitution for the establishment of World Government. All these years the U.S. government had been claiming that by renouncing my citizenship I had made myself "excludable." But how could the law "exclude" a person, even one who was "stateless," from returning to his original homeland? The nation-state was trapped in an unresolveable contradiction. For a World Citizen born in the United States, laws governing expatriation and expulsion were null and void. I was certain that I would not and could not be deported. Instead, my case opened up a Pandora's Box, exposing the dichotomy of natural rights and the delegated powers of states.

The U.S. Supreme Court nevertheless denied my petition. Early in 1982, the Court also refused to hear my petition for a rehearing, in which I claimed that world citizenship was the only way for Americans to protect their inalienable rights from the unilateral nuclear decisions of the president. After almost five years, I had reached the end of a legal journey.

According to U.S. courts, there was little doubt: I was in the country allegally. Just five minutes from the White House, an "excludable alien" was coordinating the activities of a corporation whose main work was the development of World Government, a government the Court refused to recognize. Every day this "alien" was issuing documents that Immigration bureaucrats dreaded to see.

How could they possibly let this "crime" pass any longer? According to the INS rule book, I should have been picked up immediately, and either detained forever or "excluded" — whatever that meant. What would be their next move? I wondered.

As it turned out, the government's next move was its most common: to do nothing. In spite of all their "legal" victories, they left me strictly alone. I had to ask: Who had really come out ahead? My "legal" quest was over for a while; excludable or not, I was alive and well and living in the U.S.A. But other travels lay directly ahead.

1984

Saturday, April 28

The elderly clerk behind the Northwest Orient counter at Dulles Airport was amiable enough. Still, a few trivial questions wouldn't hurt, just enough to divert his attention. If I could only manage to board the plane, I reasoned, I'd be willing to take my chances at Narita Airport Tokyo. Had my order for a vegetarian meal been received? I asked. Could I keep my seat after we reached Chicago? What was the weather in Tokyo this time of year? And, won't we be arriving on Emperor Hirohito's birthday?

Answering the questions, the clerk issued my boarding pass and directed me to the waiting room. My tactics of distraction had worked: he had forgotten to ask for a passport or visa.

For the first time since 1977, I was about to embark on an international journey. Three days earlier the Japanese Consul in Washington had refused to issue a visa based on my World Passport. But it didn't matter now. I had a round-trip ticket and a boarding pass. If I ran into trouble with Immigration in Tokyo, I could provide written invitations from Japanese educators and peace groups. And if that didn't work there were always letters of official recognition from Togo, Zambia, Upper Volta, Mauritania, Ecuador and Yemen, plus photostats of visas from over 80 countries. World Government was not short of documentation.

In preparing for the trip, I had also informed both the Japanese Emperor and the president on the United States of my intentions. In a telegram, I had congratulated Hirohito on his 83rd birthday and explained that my visit was a peace mission. To cover re-entry problems, I had written a letter to President Reagan. "I will be traveling with a World Service Authority passport, derived from Article 13(2) of the *Universal Declaration of Human Rights*," I explained. "I expect full cooperation and approval for my re-entry from the Executive Office in that you have publicly endorsed both the concept and practice of world citizenship for all Americans."

Finally, I had issued a press release, outlining my plan to register World Citizens in Japan and seek votes as a candidate for president of the world. After all, I explained, "no national candidate for public office has a program for world peace."

In traveling to the other side of the world with nothing but will-power and a World Passport, I was testing the legitimacy of World Citizenship. Would I make it? Where would these eccentric moves lead? I didn't know. I was certain, however, that responses from "high places" wouldn't make the essential difference. The most important factor was how I reacted on the ground.

What would happen when I tried to cross the Japanese and United States frontiers? It was time to find out.

Sunday, April 29

The Immigration inspector at the control booth in Narita Airport outside Tokyo took a quick look at my passport, then picked up a phone. After speaking rapidly, he motioned for me to follow him as another worker slipped into his vacated seat. A second inspector joined us in an interrogation room, looked me over, and asked politely, "Where you get this passport?"

"It's issued by our government," I explained.

"Your government? Ah so. And what government is that?"

"The World Government of World Citizens. It says so on Page 36."

"But this not national government?"

"No, it's a government based on human rights."

Mentioning human rights to an immigration official, I had often found, is like holding a cross before Dracula. No matter what they think, they cannot help but back off a bit.

In this case, the inspector also became angry. He asked why I had come to Japan. I explained that I had been invited to speak about world peace.

"You peacenik?" he asked.

"I'm a World Citizen," I replied. "Also, I am a candidate for world president. You see, your constitution is the only one in the world which renounces war. So I want to begin my campaign in Nagasaki at the Peace Park. I also have honorary World Passports for the mayors of Nagasaki and Hiroshima."

Looking them over eagerly, he asked, "But why you get no visa for Japan?"

I explained my problem with the Japanese Embassy in Washington, adding that since my tight schedule hadn't allowed enough time to resolve the issue I had decided to seek entry here, through the Ministry of the Interior. Time was short, I said. I was scheduled to be back in Washington on June 10th for a conference. Then I showed him my telex to Hirohito, a letter wishing me well from the Mayor of Washington D.C., and a press packet, including a clipping from Japan's largest newspaper, *Yomieri Shimbun*.

After listening intently, he took the material, along with my credit cards, and went off to photocopy them. When he returned, he handed back the papers.

"You cannot enter Japan," he said curtly. "You have no valid passport and no visa."

"But this is the only passport I can get," I protested. "I am stateless and this passport represents my inalienable right to travel on my home planet. After all, Japan is a member of the United Nations. According to the Charter, all Member-States are obliged to respect and observe fundamental human rights. Your refusal to let me into Japan is a violation of the right to travel."

He wasn't swayed. "We have strict regulations," he said. "No one allowed into Japan without national passport and Japanese visa. No exceptions."

Earlier that day I had bought a copy of the *Japan Times*. On the front page was a story about the Dalai Lama, who was also arriving in Japan that day. Noting the coincidence, I asked, "What kind of passport does the Dalai Lama possess? He is as stateless as I am. He is living in North India, but doesn't hold an Indian passport. In fact, many of his Tibetan monks have been issued the same passport you are refusing. Both I and the Dalai Lama are working for peace. Are you going to allow him into Japan and not me?"

Somewhat confused by the comparison, the inspector admitted that he had no idea what documents, if any, the Dalai Lama carried. But there was a difference, he decided. "He religious man, you political man," explained the bureaucrat. "He go to Buddhist monastery, but you want go to Nagasaki."

I opened a folder and pointed out Article 9 of the Showa Constitution, the governing law of his own country. Noting that this document renounced war, I explain that I lived by the same doctrine. Tired of the discussion, he turned formal, offering me the option to appeal his decision to the Minister of Justice. Papers were quickly prepared. One document stated that my application for landing was still "pending." Until the matter was settled, however, I was to stay at the airport rest house and not to leave without permission. If I failed to comply, I could be charged with "illegal landing" and deported. The Narita Rest House was next to the terminal. Upon arrival, a desk clerk asked me to sign in. Where the register form asked for nationality, I wrote, "World Citizen." No one paid the slightest attention.

Monday, April 30

The country was celebrating a national holiday, the beginning of "Golden Week." Attempts to phone my hosts, the International Secretary of the Japan Congress Against A- and H-Bombs and Professor Hanaka at Hirosaki University, proved fruitless. The next best option, I knew, was to reach the press. Both the international and Japanese wire services were interested and asked to be kept informed about developments.

That evening the airport manager for Northwest Orient called to say that my appeal had been denied. In two hours a flight would be departing for San Francisco. I would be sent back to the U.S. at airline expense.

Later, four Northwest employees accompanied me to the front desk. Handing in my keys, I turned to leave.

Then the manager said, "Here is your bill."

"What bill?"

"Two nights plus meals," he said, smiling. "It comes to $177." Awed by the audacity, I was nevertheless prepared to counter-attack in global style. Taking out my wallet, I began counting out the sum — in World Dollar bills.

"No, no, Mr. Davis," he exclaimed, "that not money. We accept only U.S. dollars or Yen. You have credit card, yes? We take that too." "Listen," I told him, "I didn't ask to be in your hotel. I was detained here, and, incidentally, wasting valuable time. Does a prisoner pay for his detention? And look at your register. I signed in as a World Citizen. You accepted me as such. Now when I pay in world money, you don't accept me anymore. Sorry, but if you want to be paid, that's what you'll have to accept."

His reply was filled with disdain. "We cannot accept this . . . paper. This not backed by anything."

I explained that I was prepared to negotiate it for any national currency he wanted. But first he would have to accept it. Afterward he could send it to the World Government Treasury Department in Washington, D.C., from which he would receive a money order — minus a one percent transfer fee. Or he could telephone the police, explain that I had refused to pay my bill, and bring charges against me. "I will be happy to defend myself before a court of law in Tokyo," I concluded.

"No, you cannot enter Japan," he shouted. "You being flown out tonight."

"Ah so," I noted. "Then you knew I was in custody and threatened with deportation if I left this hotel. So you accept a prisoner and then dare present a bill. I ought to sue you for defrauding a World Citizen."

By now my Northwest handlers knew I had no intention of paying in any way the manager would accept. Taking the bill, they asked me to move along.

***

We arrived at the international section around 8:15 p.m., only 15 minutes before my flight was scheduled to depart. I sat down. After the Northwest manager introduced himself, I explained, "I would like to see the pilot of the plane I am supposed to be flying on."

"He is aboard plane," the man said. "Come, you must go now."

"I refuse to go any further," I said, "until I see the captain."

When he asked why, I dropped my next bomb. "Because you

want to put me aboard a commercial airplane, not a prison ship. The captain is the only law on that ship once it takes off. I want to tell him my conditions for being aboard."

"Your conditions?"

Stepping in, an Immigration official asked, "Do you refuse to go aboard the plane?"

"I don't refuse anything," I told him. "But before I go aboard, I want an understanding with the captain as to what I consider my rights on this ship."

At this point, they closed in and carried me by force onto the plane. Moments later I was rudely dumped at the feet of the captain, standing just inside the door.

Rising, I straightening out my coat and tie, regained my composure, turned to him, and said, "You have a prisoner on board your ship, captain. I am obviously not a paying passenger. In these circumstances, I am obliged to inform you that I cannot assume any responsibility for my conduct while aboard. In other words, I do not accept your authority."

At first he said, "Yes, of course," and turned away, apparently confused about my mini-insurrection. He won't buy it, I thought. No doubt the Northwest manager had described me as a nice old gentleman who would give him no trouble once on board. After all, would a man dedicated to world peace cause a small war in a crowded plane? Although my opening statement clearly didn't mesh with my previous description, I still needed to do more.

Seizing the initiative, I turned to the passengers sitting in front of me. "I have an announcement to make," I said loudly. "I am a prisoner aboard this airplane. You saw me being literally carried on by Japanese Immigration officials. This is a gross injustice. You are entitled to a peaceful, pleasant trip to the United States. . . ." By now the captain had heard more than enough. "Get him off," he barked at my bewildered captors. "He's not flying on my plane."

Back at the rest house, I strode in ahead of two young Northwest chaperones. The manager looked as if he had just seen a ghost. "My key, please?" I asked with a smile. The manager glared at my young guards in utter disbelief, but provided the key to my former room. I retired with a nod and prepared for dinner.

Tuesday, May 1

In the morning, two guards were posted outside my door. They turned out to be largely ceremonial, however, since they remained glued in place when I left for breakfast. Apparently, their orders were to "guard the room" — not its occupant.

The remainder of the morning was spent on the phone, briefing the press on the events of the previous night. Tired of the hotel's menu, I decided to have lunch at the terminal, and returned around 3 p.m. No one seemed to miss me. The guards were still in the hallway. Neither of them even acknowledged my presence as I came and went. This was noblesse oblige, Japanese-style.

At about 6 p.m. the hotel manager informed me that I was again to be put aboard the 8:30 flight to San Francisco. This time, I decided, my non-cooperation would start in the hotel room. To further complicate this arbitrary deportation, I would employ an unconventional form of nonviolent resistance: I would be naked.

When the two Northwest clerks arrived with the manager, Mr. Ling, at 7:30, I was sitting on the bed wearing only jockey shorts. Although I lacked the courage to take my tactic to the limit, my state of undress was fairly effective. They were embarrassed and appalled, unprepared either emotionally or psychologically to dress a 62-year-old man with sound arguments for why he should be admitted into the country and strong objections to the injustice of the state's bureaucratic refusal. They pleaded with me to dress myself. I responded by asking to speak with the captain over the telephone, suggesting this might save us all some trouble.

A rambling conversation with Mr Ling drifted between threat and negotiation. After mentioning the police, he explained several times that he was only doing his job. If I cooperated, he promised, the pilot would decide what to do.

My deportation order was unjust, I replied. He and the airline were forcing me onto a plane against my will. "Any free, reasonable man must protest such treatment," I explained.

It was 8:15 by now, and the walkie-talkie carried by one of the airline clerks was screeching. Frustrated and angry, Ling gave an order. Startled into action, the men began forcing me into my socks and pants. Unwilling to push resistance over the border to violence, I went along. A few minutes later, half-dressed, with a suit jacket draped over my bare shoulders, I was carried down the hotel hall and through the lobby, then placed on a van.

***

At the terminal, I was hauled onto a wheel-chair and taken quickly to the most deserted part of the building, surrounded by at least ten Immigration officials and a dozen airport policemen. This time they were taking no chances.

The wheelchair stopped moving in front of the steps to the plane. I didn't move. Prepared for resistance, the clerks carried me on. Looking around, I saw no captain; he had been cleverly sequestered in the first-class cocktail lounge at the top of a narrow spiral staircase. There was no way they would carry me up there.

During the day, however, I had worked on a declaration for the other passengers. Now was the moment to test its effect.

"Ladies and gentlemen," I said, "you are witnessing an act of modern piracy. As you note, I have no wish to fly on this aircraft. I am doing all I can to prevent it." A clerk tried to muzzle me with a blanket, but I shook it off. "You too have the right to protest this wanton kidnapping at your expense. If you agree that I not fly with you, make your protest now both to the captain and to Northwest Orient personnel, both of whom are colluding in this injustice. . . ."

From the inner reaches of the cocktail lounge, a voice thundered down. "I've heard enough," shouted the captain. "Get him off my plane, pronto!"

Shrugging off my captors with as much dignity as I could muster, considering my attire, I walked off the plane.

The Immigration chief was livid. "Tomorrow you go into cell!" he screamed.

"What's the charge?" I asked mildly.

There was no reply. But when my entourage returned to the rest house, the manager took one look, clapped his hand to his forehead, and scurried into his office. The bellboys laughed uproariously.

Paris, 1948 — Post World War II Europe was ready for a new political philosophy divorced from nationalism. The UN's General Assembly came to Paris and proclaimed the Universal Declaration of Human rights. The World Citizenship movement began at the same time. Newreels and mammoth meetings were our media tools.

New York, 1950 — After two tumultous years in Europe, I return to the United States for a period of contemplation and preparation for the next steps. The trip was doubly enriching because of my first encounter in mid-Atlantic with the South Indian sage, Guru Nataraja

London, 1953 — En route to India at the invitation of Guru Nataraja, the South Indian Sage, I stepped off in London to play in "Stalag 17." the play closed after one week and I was stranded with no money or right to work. On the basis of the UDHR, I petitioned Queen Elizabeth and waited outside Buckingham Palace for a reply. After I spent nine weeks in Brixton prison, the British deported me back to the United States.

New Delhi, India, 1956 — I am administered the Oath of Allegiance to World Government at the Birla Mandir temple by a disciple of Guru Nataraja the day after my Indian visa expired.

Hannover, Germany, 1957 — During my crusade, I have been jailed 34 times by national police for not possessing "proper" documents. While in this Hannover jail allegedly for crossing from East to West Germany illegally, the city authorities nevertheless issued to me a *Fremdenpass* (foreignor's passport) which ironically identified me as "Coordinator of World Government"!

Washington, 1960— Joan Baez, renowned singer and peace activist, receives a World Passport at the National Press Building. The entertainment world, from which I came, like the sports world, accepts naturally, enthusiatically and with enormous heart the concept that "We are the world."

Vilnius, Lithuania, 1990— Twelve days after Lithuania declared its independence , while Soviet tanks rumbled through the streets and army
helicopters circled overhead, I presented an honorary World Passport
to President Vytautas Landsbergis at the nightly press conference at
the parliament house attended by more than 200 journalists.

Prague, 1989 — Vaclav Havel was intrigued with the World Passport I
presented to him when I visited him shortly after he became president
of Czechoslovakia. "Since becoming president," he told me, "they took
away my ordinary passport but didn't give me anything in return. So
this is my first passport as president! It is a most precious document."

Tokyo, 1990 — Nobel Peace Prize-winner Andrei Sakharov was the honored guest at the Nobel Laureate Forum in Tokyo, sponsored by the Yumieri Shimbun newspaper. He accepted with enthusiasm his World Passport agreeing at the same time to support the world constitutional conventions we planned for the decade 1991-2000.

Moscow, 1990 — The first official act of the newly-elected Moscow mayor Gavrill Popov was to receive a World Passport from me during my visit to the Soviet Union on my return to Tokyo .

Wednesday, May 2

This day, clearly, would be different. Though I was unguarded, I had been threatened with jail. And for the first time Northwest Orient had kept my papers and luggage at the terminal. If yesterday had been my last day of freedom, I concluded, I'd better make the most of the moment.

At 4 a.m., therefore, I dressed, walked down the back stairway, crept under the security office window, and stepped onto the street. As I walked briskly down the road away from the terminal, the early morning cold seeped through my thin shirt. Sleepy guards were stationed at various entry points to side roads. Jogging past, I paid them no attention.

Far ahead a huge gate blocked the road. On the left side was a tiny guard post. Could this airport be closed? I wondered. Then I recalled a protest I had heard about. Disturbed about the noise over nearby farmland, thousands of farmers and students had once tried to prevent this place from opening.

When I was about 50 yards away, a guard opened the gate and a truck drove through. Before he could close it I shouted, "Wait a minute." A second guard stepped out with a submachine gun in his hands. Before he could speak, I said, "What time does the airport open?"

"Six."

"Can I go through now?" I asked with a smile.

"Where you stay?"

"Narita Rest House."

"Where your passport?"

"Back at the rest house," I motioned, still smiling.

With the gate partly open, the two guards debated what to do. Gesturing as if I were a smoker, I added, "Need cigarettes. Is that Shell station open?" They still weren't sure. Moving closer, I touched one guard's shoulder, and said, "Don't worry, pal. I'll be right back." Then, without waiting for a reply, I walked out. As I sauntered down the road, I heard the gate close behind me.

At the first red light I crossed to a Hilton Hotel, hailed a taxi and jumped in.

***

At Narita Station, I bought a ticket for the Ginza, Tokyo's famous shopping area, and sat down to sweat out the next 20 minutes. It was 5:40 a.m. The guards at the gate wouldn't blow the whistle, I surmised, and at 6 they would be relieved. Immigration probably wouldn't come for me until 8. With luck I had a two hour head start.

At the Ginza, I waited for a coffee shop to open. By 9:30 I reached Christine Chapman, a correspondent for the *International Herald Tribune* to whom I'd spoken the day before. We agreed to meet at the Foreigner's Press Club for an interview and lunch. On her advice, I spent the evening at the International House of Japan at Roppongi.

Thursday, May 3

The tale of my escape appeared in the *Yomieri Shimbun* and the *Japan Times*. However, since the accounts were superficial, I decided, with some trepidation, to give the papers the whole story.

When I showed up unannounced at the main offices of the *Yomieri Shimbun*, the editors were amazed. After introductions, they showed me to a small room, where I spent the next hour answering questions about my mission, who I knew in Japan, the history of world citizenship, and what the Japanese people could do for world peace. The two young reporters assigned to me were attentive, but did more listening than writing. To compensate I provided an "open letter" composed that morning.

The telephone rang. Answering it, one of the reporters glanced at me several times during his conversation. Instantly alarmed, I knew this meant it was time to go, fast. But then, when he advised me to return to the airport and surrender, I knew it was already too late.

***

Half a block from the newspaper office I was surrounded by four men with hard eyes, one of whom flashed an Immigration badge. After a stop at the hotel to pay the bill and pick up my things, we were off to the airport. Were they still trying to deport me, I wondered, or did they have other plans?

Control was airtight as we drove past the terminal and entered a side road. We were heading down, right under the building. An Immigration cellblock, I guessed, hidden from public view.

At least ten men in uniform awaited my arrival. My interrogation was about to begin. The charge, they explained, was entering Japan illegally, a crime that carried a 30 day prison sentence. There would be no trial and therefore no defense; just the charge from the Ministry of Justice, the conviction, and the sentence. The only loose end was where I would serve my term— "inside" or "outside" Japan. Running through my catalog of defenses, I mentioned arbitrary detention without due process, the UN Charter and the *Declaration of Human Rights*. No reaction. I threatened to sue for a writ of habeas corpus. Blank stares.

"I'm a stateless person," I explained exasperated. "I have no nationality. Besides, the United States government says I am an excludable alien. In other words, I cannot re-enter the U.S." "Why you come to Japan?" my interrogator asked. Apparently he hadn't read my file.

Once more I explained why I did not accept Japan's refusal to let me enter. He recorded my fulsome arguments with a suspiciously small number of Japanese characters, then passed the matter on to the next official. This one announced proudly, "I am deciding Immigration official. Proper investigation just concluded. My decision is, you are refused to enter Japan."

"No kidding?"

"What is kidding?" After a co-worker explained it, he gave me a withering look and asked if I wanted to appeal to a "higher officer." Of course I did. But the "higher officer," it turned out, was the older man standing two feet to his right. Well, at least there were no transportation costs, I thought, and no delay between trials. The efficiency of the procedure would be an object lesson to courts throughout the world.

"I explain procedure," this one said. "You give me additional information. We write all down. Then appeal goes to Minister of Justice for final decision. You understand?"

"Yes," I replied, and thought to myself: then you deport me. Well, then I might as well get everything into the record.

"In my over thirty-five years as a stateless person," I began, "I have been subjected many times to the crime of omission, that is, of not possessing what various Immigration authorities of different nations consider a valid passport or identity paper. Now I face the dilemma once more. But my experience also tells me that the laws concerning passports are as flexible as they are arbitrary. In other words, other factors enter the picture which can determine whether a person is or is not granted entry. For instance, the purpose of the trip, the length of the stay, sponsorship in the country, available means and the possibility of leaving. All these factors are relevant here. I was invited, my stay is less than a month, I have money to live on and a return ticket. The only point of disagreement is the so-called validity of my passport. But the passport properly identifies me. It represents my right of freedom to travel, derived from the *Universal Declration of Human Rights*. It has been recognized by many national governments. And furthermore, decisions about passports are not subject to democratic control; they are made by ministries and then called laws."

Everything I said was miraculously transcribed in two lines of Japanese characters.

Friday, May 4

I awoke at 7 a.m. in a 6 by 14 foot cell. An hour later, breakfast arrived: fish, chopped cabbage, two pieces of buttered white bread, tomato juice and a tiny cup of jasmine tea. I explained that I was a vegetarian. When the guard asked what I ate, I mentioned rice, grains, vegetables, miso, tofu, fruits, seaweed and nuts. He said he would try. But lunch was no better: two pieces of white bread, some sort of egg batter fried around more bread, plus the juice, cabbage and tea. I mused: this menu is enough to drive me back to the U.S.

At 4 p.m. they came for me; the usual gang from Immigration and Northwest. Walking out onto a ramp, we stood near a huge 747. A special bus that could be cranked up to the plane's doorway was parked alongside. Closing in to prevent my escape, the Immigration men marched me forward. Inside the bus stood two heavy-built Americans. "Hello, Garry," said one pleasantly as I walked in. "Looks like we're going to be riding together."

"Is that so? Where are you guys from?"

"Seattle."

"Do you mean Northwest flew you out here to strong-arm me back to the States?"

"Well, I wouldn't put it that way. Let's say we're here to see that you don't get into any more trouble."

The situation was gradually becoming clear. These two guards from Flight Terminal Security Co. in Seattle had been hired by Northwest Orient and flown to Tokyo to "accompany" me. Was it legal? Could Northwest return me to the U.S. without asking where I wanted to go? Did I have rights? Or was I merely an object to be flown somewhere at the whim of the carrier?

Sensing my mood, they asked me to cooperate and said they were merely following orders. Meanwhile, the bus backed up to the plane. A platform slowly elevated us to the height of the plane's door. "Let's go, Mr. Davis," said one guard as the other moved behind me. A TV camera was filming us from below. Immigration officials and Northwest personnel watched as I was herded onto the plane. It was empty! Now I understood. Except for myself and my guards, the rear section of this plane would remain off limits. It was costly, but smart.

An hour later passengers were seated in the forward and middle rows. Stewards and stewardesses blocked the aisle to the rear. In desperation, I stood up and began to explain my plight in a loud voice. Horrified, the guards pleaded and attempted to pull me down. "I am a prisoner aboard this ship," I shouted. "I am guarded by these two hired guns. This isn't a prison ship. It's a commercial airliner. You have a right to a peaceful, uneventful trip. . . ." Then came a warning: "If you continue, I will have to tranquilize you."

I looked at the guard in amazement, then said loudly, "I have just been threatened by one of them. He said he would tranquilize me."

"Oh my God!" he exclaimed and sat down.

"This is an outrage," I continued. "Please inform the captain you do not wish to ride in this plane as long as a prisoner is aboard. . . ." But it was no use. No one paid attention. Though they were no more than 50 feet away, flight personnel stood between us. Besides, most of the passengers were Japanese and probably didn't understand English. The captain was in the cockpit, obviously aware of my plight but willing to accept Northwest's piracy.

I had done my best, but I was going "home."

Saturday, May 5

"All right, Mr. Davis, come along," said one of the six men who greeted me. The flight had landed in Seattle at 9:30 a.m., but I had been kept on board until the other passengers had disembarked. Looking up from my seat, I asked who he was.

"The Northwest Orient airport manager," he said. "Now, if you please."

Recapping the situation, I explained that there were several problems. First of all, the airline had shanghaid me. Second, I had no right to enter the U.S. And third, I didn't want to be here at the moment.

"But this flight is going to Philadelphia," he explained.

"So let it."

"But Seattle is the gateway. You have to see Immigration."

"Why?"

"Because . . . because they have to decide whether you can enter the United States."

We were getting nowhere. He talked about regulations and police. I mentioned piracy.

Soon a black policeman was striding up the aisle. "Okay, mister, let's go," he announced.

"Why?"

"Because I say so. Now move!"

"One moment," I said. "What is the U.S. code which allows you to order a stateless person off an international carrier at an international airport?"

His eyes narrowed. "Just get your things together and come with me." When I didn't move, he added that the request had come from Northwest. "I'm aware of that. But as a police officer, you follow legal codes and not the arbitrary wishes of a private carrier. All I am asking is the specific code which permits you to board this plane and force a person off."

"I'll give you the code after we get to Immigration. Now, will you come off?"

"Are you refusing to give me the code now, or is it that you don't know it?"

"I told you, I'll get it for you later. Now, let's go."

"You mean you don't really know whether there is a law or not authorizing you to order me off this plane?"

"I didn't say that, but I'm not going to stand here arguing with you. If you don't get moving, I'll move you."

"Are you threatening me with violence?"

"I'm threatening you with. . . ." Then he stopped, took in the looks of the Northwest management, and turned conciliatory. "Now mister," he went on, as if I was some madman he had to humor, "I don't want no trouble and I'm sure you don't either. Let's just go into the lounge and talk this over, shall we?"

I asked for his name and number, then turned to the Northwest manager and asked for his.

"Nysox," he said, his voice dripping with venom.

"You are a witness, Mr Nysox," I said, "that the police officer would not or could not give me the U.S. code authorizing this forced action."

With that, I rose and walked off the ship.

***

The Immigration section was crowded with people — Filipinos, Japanese, Mexicans, Central Americans, and more. All had some visa or entry problem. One Immigration man tried to cope with them while another snapped their pictures.

After a five minute wait, a female INS officer was ready for my case. "May I see your passport please?" she asked.

"Why? Are you going to stamp it?"

Laughing nervously, she said, "No, I just want to see it."

"There really is no need," I explained. "I'm not a U.S. citizen, nor an immigrant, nor a transient, nor a visitor. So I can't enter the United States, can I?"

"Oh yes you can," she replied. "As a parolee."

I was shocked. Immigration was desperately dragging out the same phony status it had tried to impose on me 20 years before. Suggesting that she check her facts, I mentioned my court cases and status as an "excludable alien."

Now she was confused. "I'll have to make a phone call," she said, retreating to her office.

***

Hours passed. I waited, bored. Once, as the INS woman walked by, I motioned her over and took out my passport.

Turning the pages, she looked over my visas from Togo and Upper Volta, but said nothing. Then I handed her the brochure with photocopies of various entry visas issued on World Passports. When she came upon a U.S. visa issued in the Consulate at Buenos Aires, with an INS admittance stamp at Miami Airport, her mouth dropped open. Closing the booklet, she handed it back, and stomped away. I never saw her again.

***

That evening a Northwest official and two security guards took me to a nearby hotel. Before leaving, however, I was informed by another INS official that I would be interviewed on Monday, once they received my file from Washington.

In my room, I tried to call the Associated Press. A guard rushed over and took the receiver from my hand.

"No phone calls, Mr. Davis."

According to Mr. Nysox, I discovered, I was not to leave the room, have visitors, or make phone calls. I reminded my guard that holding me incommunicado was a First Amendment violation. In the Brooklyn Detention Facility, which normally houses up to 400 detainees, there are two floors of pay telephones, I told him. Even most prisons have pay telephones these days.

I reached for the phone again.

"Please," said the guard, "let's call Mr. Nysox first."

When I reached him on the phone, I explained the law and offered to pay for the calls. The latter, I suspected, was actually the main issue.

"In that case," he replied, "you can make outside calls."

Monday, May 7

On the sixth floor of the Federal Building, at 8 a.m., I asked the detaining officer before me why I was here. Looking over the transfer papers from Northwest, he replied, "You're here because you tried to enter the United States illegally."

It was unbelieveable. "For your information," I said, "I even refused to get off the damn plane. Northwest had to call the local police. Does that sound like illegal entry?"

Before I could go much farther, another officer came in, instructed this underling to fill out "exclusionary papers," and took me away to a small office on the first floor, where another official waited at a typewriter.

"Do you mind if I ask you a few questions, Mr. Davis?" said the bureaucrat after introducing himself as Mr. Dow.

"Yes, I do. I resent even being here. I told the first Immigration officer I saw at the airport that I have no intention of entering the United States at this time. I've been under house arrest ever since. What the hell is going on?"

"Then you refuse to answer my questions?"

"Categorically?"

He tore the paper out of the typewriter, inserted another form, and started typing furiously. I was sent back to the sixth floor.

"Do you have the air fare to go back to Tokyo?"

What a question! "I have the fare," I answered, "but I'm certainly not going to pay for a passage when I was forced to come from Tokyo. That's Northwest's responsibility."

"In that case," said the bureaucrat, "you have to have a hearing. The judge has to declare you inadmissable."

"But I never wanted to enter the U.S. in the first place."

"Where did you embark from?"

"What does that have to do with it?"

"Everything. If Northwest brought you into Japan, it's responsible for getting you back here if Japan doesn't accept you."

"Well," I explained, "though I left physically from Washington, D.C., since I was never legally admitted to the U.S. in the first place, I never left from here. So they couldn't legally bring me back." He scratched his head. "That's too much for me. Anyway, that's the way it is. Now, please come with me."

In the next room a burly Japanese-American ordered me to empty my pockets.

"What for?" I asked.

"No one goes into one of my cells with anything in his pockets."

"But why am I going into a cell?"

"That's where you're going to wait for your hearing. What do you think we're running here, a hotel? Now, empty your pockets."

***

About fifteen other men were already there when I arrived. All of us were waiting to have hearings. There were Mexicans and Guatemalans, two Nigerians, a Salvadoran and a few others from South America. A young German had just turned himself in. Out of work in Washington, he was broke and had lost his passport. Back in Stuttgart a job was waiting for him.

One of the Nigerians was finishing his studies to become an architect when his visa ran out. And one young exuberant Mexican was being deported because his American wife, jealous of his relationship with another woman, was no longer willing to sponsor him. Smiling broadly, he informed me, "I will be back in six days. Then I pay $60, get a divorce, and get married with my girlfriend." Inside the large cell-block, I soon experienced the comradeship of prison buddies. The iron bars were an automatic equalizer. An immigration jail is special, however, since its victims, a world community in microcosm, are all caught "between" nations. I felt right at home.

At first they were skeptical about my World Passport and other documents. Could such things really exist? they wondered. I began to explain their rights as human beings.

"But who issues them?" asked a Mexican.

"Our own government," I replied. "You are all world citizens, but you must claim it. Then you give yourself a legal status above these national officials. You see, they don't recognize human beings, but they do recognize documents."

"Then what are you doing here with us?" the Salvadoran asked cagily.

"I am deliberately confronting national governments with my world passport. By declaring it not valid, the Japanese government actually recognized it. In other words, they had to recognize its existence, then take a stand."

"Does it cost anything?"

"Of course. We aren't rich — or philanthropists. We provide a popular service."

A few of them were almost ready to take the plunge.

NOTICE TO APPLICANT FOR ADMISSION
DETAINED FOR HEARING BEFORE IMMIGRATION JUDGE

To Garry Davis   May 7, 1984

PLEASE TAKE NOTICE THAT you do not appear to me to be clearly and beyond a doubt entitled to enter the United States as you may come within the exclusion provisions of Section 212(a) 20 & 26 of the Immigration and Nationality Act, as amended, in that you are an immigrant applying for admission to the United States and you are not in possession of a valid unexpired immigrant visa, border crossing card or re-entry permit. You are also not in possession of a valid unexpired non-immigrant visa. Therefore you are detained under the provisions of Section 235(b) of the Immigration and Nationality Act, as amended, for a hearing before a Immigration judge to determine whether or not you are entitled to enter the United States or whether you shall be excluded and deported. During such hearing you will have the right to be represented by counsel and to have a friend or relative present. AT THE HEARING BEFORE THE IMMIGRATION JUDGE YOU MUST ESTABLISH THAT YOU ARE ADMISSABLE TO THE UNITED STATES UNDER ALL PROVISIONS OF THE UNITED STATES IMMIGRATION LAWS. (Emphasis added.)

Byron P. Dow

Sitting in yet another office, I stared at the form. Was there no limit to the duplicity, or the outright stupidity? So, this was the document that Dow had been so energetically typing.

"Please sign at the bottom," an officer instructed.

"Wait a minute!" I said. "I never applied for admission to the United States as an immigrant. It's a lie. And you want me to sign this?"

"Just explain it to the hearing officer."

"Why should I have to explain it? I mean, by what right do you people deliberately falsify a document being presented to an Immigration judge and then have the gall to ask me to sign it?" He ignored the question. "It's OK if you don't sign. But it'll go into your record as being uncooperative."

"And what about Mr. Dow? He wrote it when I told him exactly the opposite? Did he cooperate with me? Will his record say that he made a false statement?"

"Let's go, Davis," he said. "Back to the cell."

***

The cell door opened, and three smiling, solicitous INS officers stepped in.

"Would you mind talking to the press?" one asked.

Ah, that was it! Now I was a celebrity. "No, not at all," I said. When we reached the hearing room, the journalists were already on hand. Two TV camera crews were setting up. I also noticed John Wiley, an Associated Press reporter with whom I had spoken several times on the phone.

The press conference lasted a half hour. Several times a hearing judge poked his head in, asking plaintively when he could have his room back. During the interview, I distributed press releases, discussed my campaign for world president, and reviewed my Japanese experience. "Why not go by the rules?" a TV reporter asked caustically. "There are no rules where I'm operating," I replied, "that is, no real laws. I am between nation-states, where there is only anarchy. All the decisions are arbitrary, from the heads of state on down. And that's why world citizenship is necessary. We insist on agreed-upon rule or, in other words, world law. That is the price of world peace." Afterward, an INS man said there would be no hearing today. My file hadn't arrived yet from Washington. In the meantime, I would be returned to a hotel in Northwest Orient's custody — under 24 hour guard.

***

To the hotel personnel at the Hyatt Regency, who only saw me with a private guard, I must have looked like some underworld top banana. That may explain why, when I requested a typewriter or photocopying facilities, they were quickly furnished free of charge. This was more than mere innkeeper hospitality.

But on Friday, when a bill for phone calls was presented, they discovered the truth. I insisted that my calls be separated from those made by my guards. After that, when press people and my secretary in Washington tried to contact me, their calls were turned away. Finally, a hearing date was scheduled: Monday, May 14. Over the weekend, Immigration again took charge, and locked me up at the Renton City Jail.

Monday, May 14

This hearing might be the culmination of seven years of legal tests. Hopefully, I could finally prove my point, made originally on May 25, 1948: the individual has an inalienable right to choose his or her political allegiance, and national institutions simply have to recognize it. In May, 1977, the U.S. Justice Department had claimed that I was "excludable" from the country of my birth. Now the Immigration and Naturalization Service would have to decide whether I could remain in the U.S. as a World Citizen.

If the government claimed that I was an "excludable alien subject to deportation" and yet did nothing about it, my innate sovereignty as a human being was being implicitly recognized. That, in turn, would legitimize my claim to world citizenship. My sovereignty would overrule the sovereignty of the nation-state.

***

Judge Newton Jones called the hearing to order. After reviewing the facts, he suggested that I might want a lawyer.

"Your honor," I said, "I don't need counsel because I have no defense." With that introduction, I reviewed Dow's fraudulent letter and my alien status, as determined by other courts. The INS lawyer, Mr. Hopkins, was forced to agree.

"But I have to make a determination," the judge injected, a bit perplexed. "You're in my jurisdiction."

"I'm in your jurisdiction because I was forced into it," I said. "I'm not here of my own free will. I was shanghaid out of Toyko by Northwest Orient."

"But the Japanese government wouldn't accept you."

"Are you basing your determination on what another nation does or doesn't do?" I asked. "I was under the impression that the United States of America and Japan were two separate sovereign governments."

"They are," he replied testily, "but if the Japanese government didn't accept you — that is, if you didn't legally enter onto foreign soil, then according to U.S. law, let's see, *Kaplan vs. Todd,* you never left the United States."

I reminded the judge that, in fact, both governments had refused me admittance. How could I have left the U.S., I asked, when I was never admitted in the first place?

"It's quite a dilemma," he said, leaning back in his chair.

For Hopkins, however, the issue was simple. "Mr. Davis is inadmissable, period," he said. "The Justice Department has always maintained that position."

Again I agreed; the hearing was simply irrelevant.

The judge looked grim. What could he do? If he declared me inadmissable, the INS would have to turn me over to Northwest, which would then be obliged to fly me back to Japan. On the other hand, if he declared me admissible, even though I was neither a citizen, immigrant or visitor, he would be implicitly recognizing my world citizenship claim.

Was I about to prove that inalienable rights are truly global? Judge Jones took a paper from his desk. "I will now read into the record," he said, "the text of a telex received today from Immigration and Naturalization Service in Washington D.C. Quote: The file on Mr. Garry Davis has been lost. Unquote."

I stared at him. Lost? A file dating back to 1950. A controversy that reached as far as the U.S. Supreme Court. By this time it must be ten meters long. Lost? It was simply not believeable. Of course, the INS office in Washington was hopelessly inefficient. Files were packed in cartons stacked up to the ceilings. But this sounded more like a cover-up — or a cop-out.

Moving on, Judge Jones recapped the case and made his decision. "I hereby determine," he said, "that you never left the United States and that you are in the same legal status now that you were on April 28, 1984. Case closed."

That was it! A U.S. judge had, in effect, sanctioned my status as a World Citizen. How? By stating that I never left the United

States, he was also saying that I had a right to be in the country. According to the INS, I had never been admitted. But according to the judge, I'd never left. When Judge Jones said "the same legal status," that actually meant "excludable alien," inadmissable, get out. But the case was closed, my file was lost, and the INS, as usual, did nothing — that is, except take me to the airport and wave goodbye.

Thirty-six years to the day after leaving for Europe to renounce my nationality, I had finally, officially, come home. I had left as a U.S. citizen and returned as a citizen of the world.

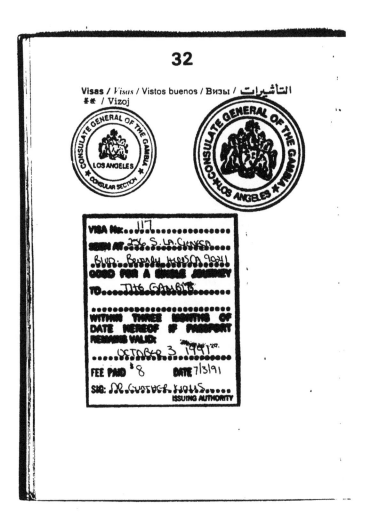

The Global Contract

Chapter 23

Searching for Higher Authority

"As long as there are sovereign nations possessing great power, war is inevitable. There is no salvation for civilization, or even the human race, other than the creation of world government."
—Albert Einstein

"The creation of an authoritative all-powerful world order is the ultimate end towards which we must strive. Unless some effective world super-government can be set up and brought quickly into action, the prospects for peace and human progress are dark and doubtful."
— Winston Churchill, Prime Minister, Great Britain

"There exists a growing body of international law which is normally observed in the relations between nation states, although there can be no codification of this until there is an accepted World Government. There is not, however, a World Authority capable of enforcing International Law."
—Julius Nyerere, President, Tanzania

"The time has come . . . to supplement balance of power politics with world order politics."
—Jimmy Carter, President, United States

Bold proposals to prevent war and enlarge the scope of human freedom have been advanced for centuries. Even before the industrial revolution transformed aggression from a regional tragedy into a global threat, philosophers and politicians had begun to look and think beyond the borders of their nations.

For the French revolutionist Jean Baptiste Du Val-De-Grace, the answer, in 1792, was a World Republic that would place human rights above the rights of individual states. All peoples would have cultural autonomy, he imagined, yet all national boundaries would be abolished. Three years later, the German Philosopher Immanuel Kant proposed a more modest plan: a confederation of nations. Urging world citizenship and freedom of movement, Kant hoped that a "covenant of peace" would ultimately make national conflict obsolete.

Throughout the next hundred years, diplomats and statesmen struggled with formulas for transnational order. Finally, in 1899, on the initiative of Czar Nicholas, an agreement — The Hague Treaty — between 24 major states was reached. Recognizing that modern warfare and weapons posed a threat to all humanity, the nation-states pledged at least to attempt settling their differences through "pacific methods" rather than force and violence.

Ten million people died during World War I anyway.

The massive violence of that conflict was a sign that few nations could ignore. In the aftermath, treaties outlawing war were signed, and the League of Nations was established. Like confederal plans before it, however, the League was complex and largely ineffective, both burdened with responsibilities and deprived of real authority. Despite human rights declarations dating from 1789 in France, the League still represented only states, with no allusion in its charter to the sovereignty of ordinary people much less humanity. Within four years after its founding in 1919, it inevitably began to split into hostile alliances.

During the next "world war," 60 million people died, more than half of them civilians, and in 1945 the "nuclear age" crashed into existence when atomic bombs were dropped on two Japanese cities. The very nature of war had become global. The survival of humanity was now at stake. The nation-state war game, however, continued unabated. By this time, the concept of world government could no longer be shrugged off as some utopian novelty. The possibility of nuclear warfare had made the choice all too clear: global order or oblivion. But what kind of order? The United Nations, launched within that same fateful year, 1945, was more like a forum than a government. It could not legislate on worldwide problems, nor enforce its views through any means but military action. Its members, all nation-states, still remained absolutely sovereign, free to make treaties or declare war without even a nod to the UN.

National citizenship became a collective suicide pact.

Over the next four decades, whenever UN decisions or Charter provisions stood in the way of some "national" desire, they were routinely ignored. As the Cold War gave birth to the nuclear arms race, as more than 150 armed conflicts between nations "great" and "small" created millions more victims, it became all too clear that this latest attempt to create peace through a confederation of nation-states was no more than a sterile exercise in futility. War, deprivation and torture gave grim daily testimony to the fact that the UN was virtually powerless to protect and promote peace or human rights. Could it be any other way? Was it even possible for sovereign nations to surrender the right to "defend" themselves through war? Writing as the United Nations Charter was being designed in 1945, Emery Reves provided an answer: war was avoidable only if some "higher" legal order was imposed. In *Anatomy of Peace*, he explained:

> The real cause of war has always been the same. They have occurred with a mathematical regularity of a natural law at clearly determined moments as a result of clearly definable conditions . . . 1. Wars between groups of men forming social units always take place when these units — tribes, dynasties, churches, cities, nations — exercise unrestricted sovereign power. 2. Wars between social units cease the moment sovereign power is transferred from them to a larger or higher unit. . . ." In other words, ". . . Wars always ceased when a higher unit established its own sovereignty, absorbing the sovereignty of the conflicting smaller social units.

So long as the nation-state's self-imposed amnesia persists, other wars are inevitable. Like previous attempts to "rationalize" conflict without a fundamental transfer of sovereign power, the UN can only succeed in isolated cases, when armed conflict no longer serves the selfish interest of the belligerents. Mainly, it is a hostage — politically and financially — of the system it is expected to transform.

But if the confederal approach is not the form of "higher authority" that can break nationalism's spell, moving us to a workable and democratic world order, what is?

***

We live in a geocentric world of nation-states, preoccupied mainly by "national" problems of the economy, society and politics. No matter where we live, for most of us the "nation" is the center of our political universe — the immovable point around which revolve all other nations and, supposedly, the rest of the world.

Our attachment to our nation is not merely legal; it is profoundly emotional. Yet when nations deal with other nations, these attachments are given no weight. In the usual "inter--national" context, the individual is nowhere to be found. Still, all nations claim to represent the very people they so often ignore. Ironically, most nations claim to derive their very legitimacy from their citizens. But if individuals — the people themselves — are truly the source of each nation's authority, it follows that humanity as a whole rather than any nation is the highest source of authority. Thus, the accumulated power of nation-states does not make them the only legitimate participants in global decision-making. In a world threatened by war and injustice, "responsible citizenship" can only mean a powerful assertion of humanity's ultimate sovereignty. As Thomas Paine explained it, "individual human beings, each in his or her own personal and sovereign right, enter into a compact with each other to produce any government." For a "higher authority" to come into being, therefore, a new compact is needed, a global civic contract that transcends the national paradigm.

***

The good news is: that contract already exists . . . both naturally and legally.

World Government, which was established in 1953, is both an extention of the individual and an expression of humanity as a whole. It grows from your sovereignty and mine as world citizens, and from our commitment to each other's protection and survival. It is a horizontal network based on both our natural rights, and the human rights affirmed by both national constitutions and international agreements like the *Universal Declaration of Human Rights*. It is also "vertical" as the political expression of a world community by those who recognize only the geographic limits of the planet itself.

In 1945, while observing delegates at the founding of the UN in San Francisco, E. B. White wrote: "Whether we wish it or not, we may soon have to make a clear choice between the special nation to which we pledge our allegiance and the broad humanity of which we are born a part." World Citizens are those who have made the choice.

In a more practical sense, World Government is an outgrowth of the world citizenship movement that began in the late 1940s. At the start, World Government was simply a tool, a way to embody the transnational civic identity that was being adopted by the many people who registered as World Citizens beginning in 1949. Gradually, however, it became more: an embryonic structure for the evolution of a global civism. Once its administrative arm, the World Service Authority, was established in 1954, the first full phase of its work began. The WSA began identifying people from all corners of the planetary community, issuing documents to those who pledged their allegiance to the World Government of World Citizens.

Over the years since that official beginning, World Government has aimed at overcoming the psychological barriers imposed by the polarized, dualistic nation-state system. In one sense, its very existence and the documents used by its citizens expose the anti-democratic core of most nation-states. But for many people — refugees and other outcasts of the system — its value is more basic. For them, World Government means global political asylum.

At this point, it is still largely a service organization. But it is also a way for people to take a step onto solid new ground. By joining with others as part of this evolving government, World Citizens send a signal of world unity, penetrating public consciousness in subtle but profound ways. Each time a person sees the dynamic relationship between his/her individual identity and humanity, the nation-state has lost a subject. Each time someone crosses a frontier with a World Passport, the mythic sovereignty of the nation is exposed.

Within the conceptual framework of World Government, the universal elements of religious teachings and democratic political and legal theories converge. It represents a holistic way of thinking about oneself and the planet. The deeper one goes, the more profound the potential transformation can be.

Today our world remains deafened by the roar of chaos and conflicting loyalties. Once the possibility of an alternative has been envisioned, however, it quickly becomes obvious that the primary causes of the chaos are the nation-states themselves. National governments cannot solve our problems. They are the problem.

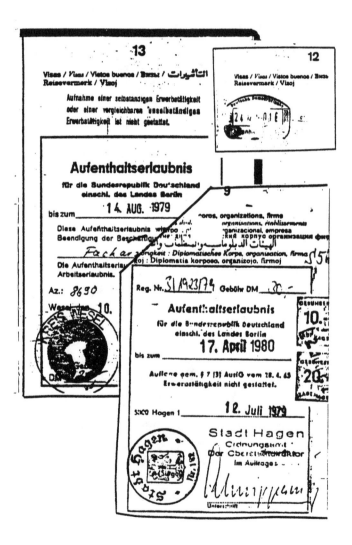

Chapter 24

What Is World Government?

You might say that World Government had already been in existence for five years before it was officially founded. In 1948, by declaring myself a world citizen, I had taken the first essential step. Over the next year, more than a half million people from over 150 countries signed up at the International Registry of World Citizens which evolved from that initial gesture. And when the United States allowed me to enter the country on my return from France in 1950, it moved the process further along by recognizing my sovereignty. In a sense, I had become a global legal entity.

But that did not prevent other national governments from ignoring the unique status. Though 125,000 Germans had registered as World Citizens by 1950, Bonn refused to let me in that year while I camped on the border at Pont Kehl at Strasbourg. When I visited England to appear in a play three years later, the reception was even less hospitable: I was denied a work permit, thrown into Brixton Prison for 9 weeks, and shipped back to the U.S. on a fraudulent deportation order. Needless to say, I was boiling mad.

After that jail experience, my 16th, the path was clearer than ever. World Citizens needed something more than general principles if we were to be taken seriously. We needed a pragmatic, legal basis from which to deal with national bureaucrats. It wasn't enough to assume World Government; we would have to proclaim it.

From the eminent civil rights lawyer, Arthur Garfield Hayes, I learned that, in order to warrant recognition by other governments, World Government would have to be formally declared.

It would need some guiding principles, and would have to fill a need. At this early stage, a constitution wasn't required. And our government needn't have territory, though it could claim some. By extending that territorial claim to the entire planet, however, World Government could then claim the authority to register citizens, issue birth certificates and passports, and even print money.

Why not? I concluded. There was nothing to lose and literally a world to win.

How It Began

On September 4, 1953, before a small audience in the town hall of Ellsworth, Maine, the World Government of World Citizens was born. It drew its powers and prerogatives, I explained in my declaration, from three prime laws: one God, one world, and one humankind. Though I was merely one person, all humans were potential World Citizens. They need only claim their rights and assume their responsibilities. "A presumptuous undertaking?" I asked. "Not at all, for nothing less will serve us, and we must risk being called presumptuous by narrow minds and closed hearts. I will answer that all newborns are presumptuous in their demands for sustenance and attention." In order to grow, this newborn government would need many forms of sustenance: a constituency, an economy, and the contributions of scientists, managers, technicians and artists. Over time it could tackle the problems of food, shelter, clothing, health, education, labor, production and distribution of resources that were troubling the planet. The start, however, would be modest: a simple statement of World Government's intent — and some way to get it organized. Six months later, the World Service Authority was founded in New York as the administrative arm of World Government. It would be a non-profit, global "city hall" for anyone helping to evolve World Government and anyone who needed this government's help. Coordinating all World Government activities, the WSA would implement human rights, develop other agencies and services, and provide a documentation service. The burgeoning demand for global documents — passports, identity cards, and so on — from refugees and other World Citizens was more than a single person could handle. The WSA office, drawing its authority from the *Declaration of Human Rights*, would make World Government operational. It would institutionalize the concept and develop the constituency.

Since 1954, the World Service Authority has issued more than 350,000 passports, as well as a variety of other identity documents. It is a non-profit corporation, with offices in Washington, D.C. and Toyko, and agents throughout the world. If the rights of a registered World Citizen are violated, the WSA takes up the defense. Operating above the level of the individual nation-state — on the "meta" level — it confronts governments and bureaucrats with their defiance of world law. In countless cases, refugees have succeeded in remaining in the country of their choice with WSA intervention. As mentioned previously, more than 100 nations recognize World Government on an "unofficial" basis by allowing holders of WSA documents to pass through their frontiers. The name of the corporation itself makes the purpose clear. Its scope is the world. Its task is service — that is, what any government ought to provide for its citizens. And its "authority" is the sovereignty of the individual, the only way to transcend the paper power of the nation-state.

For many stateless people, World Government represents the only haven from the hostility of bloodless and indeed heartless nation-states. For anyone working for human rights and world peace, it can be still more: a way to create a true global community, to make nationalism obsolete and legalize the already existent humanity.

How It Works

World Government IS humanity. It does not demand the surrender of any freedom, the renouncing of "national" citizenship, or any disloyalty whatsoever to the nation of one's birth. Rather it replaces the anachronistic political system that emerged in the 18th Century with a global contract that recognizes the dynamic interdependence of our time. We are already linked across our artificial frontiers; neither mass communications, science, commerce, nor ecology recognizes national borders. In these areas and many more, we already have one world. All types of barriers are crumbling. World Government makes our politics consistent with our reality.

As it has evolved, the World Government of World Citizens has responded to the needs of its Citizens not only by issuing documents such as birth and marriage certificates, visas and passports. It has also begun to establish other basic organs of government: study commissions and a court, a political party, police force and monetary system.

The World Court of Human Rights, for example, was established in France by a General Assembly of World Citizen delegates in 1972. Subsequently, a provisionary statute for the court was drafted, and still later the World Judicial Commission was set up to handle preliminary complaints filed by World Citizens. The International Court of the Hague, we had discovered, only handles cases between sovereign states, and only if both parties agree to the litigation. The UN Commission on Human Rights is powerless to help individuals when their freedom and the arbitrary will of a nation-state collide. In particular, World Citizens, whose exercise of human rights often contravenes "national laws," need a new kind of court, one both grounded on the legal defense of global rights and accessible to all. As the first Chief Justice of this Court, Dr. Luis Kutner, explained upon accepting the post, "The international community has come to realize that human rights are not an issue to be left solely to the national jurisdiction of individual states. These rights obviously need protection at a higher level within the framework of international law."

Over the years, a variety of study commissions have also been formed to deal with specific global problems. Experts, all advocates of a just and democratic world order, have been recruited to pursue research in areas such as health, space, culture, economics, education, women, forestry, political asylum, communication and cybernetics. And in 1987, a World Citizens party was launched in Washington, D.C. to provide an electoral vehicle of empowerment for World Citizens.

Unlike most governments, which are heavily in debt, World Government is self-financing. Citizens who request services pay modest fees to cover its operating expenses. The World Refugee Fund and World Citizens Legal Fund help to finance travel documents for refugees, displaced persons and political prisoners, and to pursue legal cases for citizens whose rights have been violated or who face prosecution under national laws. World Government also has its own currency and embryonic banking system.

The World Service Authority Passport remains, of course, the most widely used document, a practical symbol and a useful tool for travelers. Major contributors to the World Refugee Fund, who receive a deluxe leather-bound passport, make it possible to issue passports for free to many refugees and war victims, half of them women and children. In essence, World Government is a sustainable and self-sufficient community of sovereign individuals who have given their prime allegiance to an emerging body of "common world law," including various human rights covenants, the Stockholm Environmental Declaration and the Nuremberg Principles. It is neither a parallel government nor a supra-national federation. It is a "meta-government" of individual human beings.

Chapter 25

A Non-Military Alternative

"No one shall be held in slavery or servitude . . ."
— Article 4, *Universal Declaration of Human Rights*

U nder the rules of most war-prone nations, conscription of young men and, sometimes, women — or at least strong enticement — into the armed forces is legal and logical. Murder is a crime, yet training to kill and killing itself is called patriotism. The contradiction between the social code enforced within most countries and the code governing relations between nations could barely be more flagrant or tragic. The killing of soldiers by other soldiers is rewarded with medals and promotions. In some nations, soldiers are even ordered to quell civic rebellions by their own countrymen and women, told that a protest against some despotic government is actually a subversive, warlike engagement. To refuse to be conscripted or to fight will be met, in most places, with a prison term. The unwilling victim will then, ironically, probably be placed in confinement with murderers.

Conscription nevertheless violates several forms of international law. Under the Nuremberg Principles, "any person who commits an act which constitutes a crime under international law is responsible therefore and liable to punishment." These crimes include planning, preparing, initiating or waging a war of aggression. A standing national army, which is inherently a threat to other armies, is a per se violation of the Principles. In addition, the implicit threat posed by standing armies violates Article 1 of the *Universal Declaration of Human Rights,* which states that human beings, born free and equal, should act toward one another "in a spirit of brotherhood." This primary human legitimacy and responsibility supercedes the secondary legitmacy known as nationality.

Yet when a young person refuses to enter a national army or stands before a military court, he is told, "Sorry, you are not a human being. You are only a national citizen, subject only to national laws or consequences." Caught without a document that attests to his humanness, he faces an untenable choice: kill for the state or go to jail.

What would help? How can law and human rights be linked to provide an alternative for the young person who refuses to kill? The answer can be found at birth, when the individual emerges into the human community from the womb. Understanding the implications, nation-states usurp this human birthright by claiming the newborn as state property. The legal principles involved are *jus soli* (where born) and *jus sanguinis* (of what parentage). On the basis of these two universal legal concepts, governments issue an exclusive document that "proves" the newborn's nationality. It is known as a birth certificate.

The baby has been born into the world, as a world citizen, not "into" a particular political fiction called a nation. Yet when the parents accept this first civic document in the name of their child, they are allowing the nation to turn a natural world citizen into a national "subject." The birth certificate becomes a form of theft, the theft of the child's true identity.

World Birth Certificate

By affixing a national seal of approval to a child, the state denies the freedom, rights and dignity guaranteed by the UN Declaration. To reclaim them, then, requires another tool, one that confirms the being's true identity as a human — a World Birth Certificate.

Once a World Birth Certificate is accepted by either the person it identifies or his or her parents, it supercedes national documents. For parents of different nationalities, a dilemma is resolved; they need not choose one nationality or another for their child. As a basic world civic identity document, the birth certificate has defined the baby's true status.

Standing before a judge, accused of refusing to serve in the military, a young person can produce a World Birth Certificate and explain that he is not permitted, under Article 30 of the *Declaration of Human Rights,* "to engage in any act aimed at the destruction of any of the rights and freedoms set forth herein." Furthermore, he or she can claim to be subject to, and the subject of, international law. A World Birth Certificate can also be used as the basis for refusal to pay war taxes. Thus, World Citizenship, combined with proof of identity, can help to neutralize the state's power to coerce.

World Guards

Normally, the police officer is a public servant, one who is expected to protect and personify the common morality of the community. The soldier, on the other hand, is a state servant who obeys the arbitrary dictates of a group holding power. The former volunteers for service; the latter is often drafted for duty. Essentially, the police officer is a symbol of law, while the soldier symbolizes the state of anarchy that exists between nations.

Enforcing world law, however, is substantially different from seeing that laws of a local or national nature are obeyed. Violations at the global level — making or preparing for war, violating basic human rights, polluting the environment — are crimes against humanity itself, the entire species. They cannot be stopped or redressed by more violence. In essence, such crimes are manifestations of mental illness at the mass level. Only by dealing with the mental, emotional or material causes can the cycle of violence be halted.

This work calls for "World Guards" who combine the qualities of an Old West Sheriff, Indian sage and Robin Hood. World Guards act as direct representatives for World Citizens whose rights are violated, settling disputes between individuals and attacking national ignorance, intolerance and hypocrisy. Physically unarmed, they are roving ombudsmen who attempt to put wisdom to work for the benefit of humanity. The idea is to speed the process of justice, which is often excessively expensive and long, and to make certain that human rights are defended.

For the unwilling recruit to some national army, membership in the Sovereign Order of World Guards can be a nonviolent, constructive alternative. In fact, the idea itself, like many other aspects of World Government, evolved from such a practical problem. Shortly after my 1956 journey to India, when I first used a World Guard uniform to insulate myself from authoritative challenges, I met a 19 year old conscientious objector named Fred Haas. Told to appear before a Selective Service Board in Forest Hills, NY, Fred had filed for CO status based on his philosophical and political beliefs. His request, however, had been rejected because his reasons were not religious.

From Objection to Projection

The notion of conscientious objection, worthy as it is, is based on a continued political allegiance to one's nation-state. National law still prevails, and those who refuse either to obey or perform alternative national service can be punished. In some nations, such as Israel, where a state of continual crisis requires military service by everyone, the idea of conscientious objection is close to treason. Unfortunately, neither pacifism nor conscientious objection respond effectively to the rationale of "national security."

The key to the dilemma is a question: why are all states so insecure? Well, for nation-states, the globe is a dangerously chaotic place. Every other state is a potential enemy, and violence is always a possibility. The only way to eliminate the problem is by appealing to a higher law, a civic loyalty that provides true security by eliminating murder as an option. This new commitment becomes a conscientious projection, the acceptance of a higher civil "obedience." After becoming a World Citizen in early April, 1957, Fred Haas drafted a letter describing his new status and philosophy, and sent it to the head of his draft board, as well as to the UN Secretary-General, and President Eisenhower. On the day he was to report for his physical, he would stay home and wait to see if the draft board wished to prosecute him.

Despite his bravery, the young man was nervous. What if they sent him to jail? Would he be considered a traitor by his father, or a cop-out by his friends?

Reminding him that the worst prison is a bad conscience, I urged him to follow his truth. But at the same time, I also suggested a way to handle his critics. As a World Citizen, he could volunteer to join the World Police.

"But there is no world police force," he said.

"There will be when you sign up," I replied, and began drafting an application form for the Sovereign Order of World Guards. Upon entry, I explained, he would be trained as an world peace-keeper.

Though the draft board responded coolly to his letter, ordering him to report for induction and threatening charges of desertion if he didn't, his deadline date passed without incident. By June, his case had been passed up the Pentagon line, but still no decision. The more government lawyers studied the issue, the more intriguing — and troubling — it became.

The Sleeping Giant

This was no longer a simple CO case. First of all, there was the question of World Government: what the hell was it? That was a political issue they preferred to ignore. A second, related question was whether a U.S. citizen could pledge his allegiance to this so-called World Government. And third, if he could do it, was he still a U.S. citizen? They didn't want to get into that one either.

If Fred Haas was prosecuted as a deserter, he could bring up international law to justify his actions. The Pentagon was already having problems with the Nuremberg Principles. Lawyers for the Selective Service certainly didn't want to defend national soldiery against human rights. Of course, they were also afraid of publicity. Once the case went public, thousands of other draft-age men might try to use the same route. Even people already in jail might turn to World Citizenship as a defense. Finally, the government could not forget the international implications. In short, it was a can of global worms.

Clearly, geo-dialectical logic was at work. By pledging allegiance to World Government, Fred Haas was able to neutralize an oppressive law of his nation. His simple, sovereign act exposed just how weak the nation actually was. In *Civil Disobedience*, Thoreau had likened the state to an old lady counting her spoons — so weak it could be bent to one person's will. Sometimes the resistance of a single person can bring change to an entire government — witness Gandhi, Gorbachev, and Nelson Mandela.

But Fred hadn't won yet. Unable to decide what to do, governments often delay, perhaps hoping the problem will simply go away. In Fred's case, that was the prevailing wisdom until a constitutional lawyer working for the Pentagon provided the final argument..against the government. If Fred Haas was prosecuted, this attorney predicted, he could use the Ninth Amendment to the U.S. Constitution as his defense. Back in 1957, I wasn't quite certain what that Amendment said. Since then, however, I have spent quite a bit of time thinking about "the sleeping giant." It reads as follows:

AMENDMENT IX
The enumeration in the Constitution, of certain rights, shall not
be construed to deny or disparage others retained by the people.

Fred could simply claim that one of those rights was his right to claim a higher civic allegiance. Although there was nothing in the Constitution about delegating power to a world government, there was also nothing denying or prohibiting it. As a U.S. citizen, Fred might well have a constitutional right to delegate part of his sovereignty to a world government. This was, at the very least, a legal bombshell, one the U.S. government did not want in court.

As you might guess, Fred Haas was never prosecuted. He left for India several years later, became a disciple of Guru Nataraja, and adopted the Sannyasin way of life. Meanwhile, the ranks of World Guards continue to grow, recruited from registered World Citizen volunteers.

To determine eligibility of a potential Guard, various tests are given. You can be sure, though, that there is no discrimination based on color, national origin, gender, ethnic grouping or any other variable. Once you are accepted, of course, a registration card and badges are provided.

Chapter 26

Territory: A Worldly View

Without territory, nations would not exist. The word itself makes the matter clear: "territory" refers primarily to land and water that belongs to a particular government. As a result, unfortunately, it is used as a synonym for property. In a legalistic sense, every nation stakes its claim to "own" the piece of territory it controls. Eventually, this national territory becomes sacrosanct, and the nation girds itself to defend that "property" at all costs.

In 1991, the world witnessed the dangerous consequences of this faulty logic. Saddam Hussein's annexation of Kuwait in August, 1990 was, among other things, a brutal attempt to restore the so-called territorial integrity of Iraq. U.S. President George Bush responded by declaring war and mobilizing the broadest multinational military force in half a century — allegedly to protect the sovereignty of a sheikdom whose territorial boundaries were drawn by the British in the 1920s. Of course, most people felt that the real reason was Kuwait's oil. Saddam's subsequent attempt to link withdrawal from Kuwait with Israel's annexation of Palestinian territory illustrates just how convoluted and deadly such territorial games can become.

But do nation-states really "own" various pieces of the planet? For centuries, they have usurped control over larger and larger territories. Yet their continual war-making and waste demonstrates that they have no fundamental connection to the so-called property they develop, exploit and destroy. Though claiming "absolute" ownership, nation-states actually view their territory in "relative" terms, as a resource to be saved or sacrificed, seized or destroyed, depending on the requirements of "national security." Faced with Iraq's annexation, for example, the exiled Kuwaiti royal family suggested that even nuclear bombing was acceptable in the struggle to regain their territory.

In such cases, like the U.S. crusade in Vietnam, the logic is that a country might have to be destroyed in order to "save" it. Insane as it seems, nations even treat their own alleged "property" as if it were expendable. Obviously such "ownership" is no more legitimate than the primitive practice of slavery — domination in a crude disguise.

Territory can be viewed in another way, however, one which is both holistic and absolute. In the holistic sense, territory is not "property" but rather part of one great living being that includes land, sea, air and all living species. Looked at this way, destruction of territory is self-destruction, an act bordering on suicide. In the absolute sense, territory cannot be "owned" by any limited group, whether a people or a government. Everyone owns the Earth — and at the same time, no one does.

This holistical and absolute approach to the notion of territory is the basis for a revolutionary claim: that the entire surface of the planet is, in reality, world territory.

On Legal Ground

However logical, moral, even ecologically sane it may appear, you may wonder: does World Territory have any "legal" ground to stand on? It's a fair question. The definitive answer was provided when a small piece of land near the French-Swiss border was declared as a territorial base for World Government. Moving to the border community of Hesingue with my family in 1971, I had bought some land, and built a house called Chaggara. Five years later, on May 23, 1976, Chaggara became "Territoire Mondiale."

Under international law, we had discovered, not only nation-states have rights. Even before the UN was founded, other "international entities" had often been recognized — insurgent communities, governments-in-exile, religious groups claiming a territorial base, and even individuals. Perhaps the most prominent example is the Holy See, an independent Papal "state" created by the Lateran Treaty of 1929. Through this treaty, Italy recognized the sovereignty of the Holy See and its jurisdiction over the City of the Vatican. Other states have since established diplomatic relations and entered into treaties with the entity that has come to be known simply as the Vatican. Like the Vatican, Chaggara would provide an initial territorial base — in this case, a base for global political asylum. Its claim of international status was also not unique, we found. Various political developments have prompted the recognition of protectorates, mandates, associated states, and other entites. In 1920, the Free City of Danzig was created through the Treaty of Versailles as an autonomous entity under the protection of the League of Nations. The Permanent Court of International Justice held in 1932 that Danzig was a state and therefore a subject of international law. From 1920 to 1935, and again from 1947 to 1956, the "Free Territory of Trieste" was given special international status. During the second period it was an autonomous entity, although France conducted its foreign relations. Could World Government make a similar claim for the international legitimacy of Chaggara? No rule of law precluded it, and other entities had already established the precedent. The international character of World Government was clearly established, and supported by a vartiety of covenants and declarations. Taken together, these documents established six relevant principles:

- people have the right to change their nationality or to become stateless (art. 15[2], *Universal Declaration of Human Rights*);
- they also have the right to determine their own political status, along with the right to political representation (democratic principle);
- every human being has the right to choose his or her own government (*Declaration of Independence;* art. 21(3), UDHR, *inter alia*);
- the principle of self-determination is firmly established by the *Charter of the United Nations* (Preamble, art. 1)
- since individuals can be held responsible for crimes under international law, they must also be assured international rights (*Nuremberg Principles*);
- people who face political persecution have a right to global political asylum (art. 14[1], UDHR).

Given all this, the central issue was not whether a particular nation decided to recognize World Government or enter into treaties with it. That was a matter of its own choosing, based on need or circumstances. The United States, for example, chose freely to enter into an agreement with the UN to allow a permanent headquarters in New York. Wherever the UN has offices, similar agreements exist. The UN's alleged legitimacy, however, does not depend on these arrangements. Based on the nature and scope of international agreements, the main point was that, since World Government was legitimate, no concrete rule prevented it from setting up a territorial base. World territory was in no fundamental respect inconsistent with either history or any nation's law. As a qualified "international" entity, it was entitled to the same respect and recognition as any embassy. And given the desperate need for a government dedicated to the defense and implementation of human rights and freedoms, such privileges were the least to be expected.

International Homeland: 1948

The idea of world territory, like World Government itself, evolved gradually out of a variety of practical experiences. And the very first was a consequence of my initial choice to become "stateless." Though I had been able to reclaim my identity by issuing myself documents in 1948, I remained on land that was considered French territory. The government which claimed to "own" that territory wanted me out. In September, 1948, the Soviet Union had only recently consolidated its hold over Czechoslovakia. Both the State of Israel and the Republic of South Korea had just been founded, setting the stage for ongoing conflicts in Asia and the Middle East. As the world split into East and West blocs, each side made new military alliances. The world was a choatic collection of hostile and often paranoid nations. Meanwhile, in Paris, the UN General Assembly was about to meet. The session began on September 7, only four days before my deadline to leave France. If I couldn't find some way around my dilemma, imprisonment was highly likely. While glancing at a news account about the UN session, however, the solution suddenly appeared. The Palais de Chaillot, site of the meeting, had been declared "international territory." What better home could there be for a citizen of the world? On September 12, I set up camp on the Palais' steps. When asked by guards to move, I explained my reasoning: I was still in Paris, but I had "left" France and entered the UN's "international territory." For the next six days I stayed at my campsite. The media hovered as food and support poured in. A new transnational constituency was beginning to identify itself.

Eventually, the UN asked the French government to step in. Early on September 17, as flash bulbs popped my tent was torn down and I was whisked away. My first visit to "international" territory had been short-lived, but not entirely fruitless. The French authorities subsequently decided to ignore my "illegal" status, more of the world was learning about world citizenship, and, although I didn't know it at the time, the first piece of world territory was about to be declared.

Mundialization

By early 1949, over 50,000 letters of support had poured in from World Citizens around the world. Meanwhile, in the south of France, a community of 300 called Trouilla decided to become a "world town." Most of the residents had declared themselves World Citizens, and the local council had passed an ordinance warning that anyone caught making an atomic bomb on their "world territory" would be severely prosecuted. In July, another town, Cahors, asked to join the movement. With a population of 15,000, Cahors was the first major community to be officially "mundialized." No break with the French government was necessary, though a majority of the population had registered themselves as World Citizens. During a visit to Cahors, our team developed a Mundialization Charter that was accepted by the city council and approved by 70 percent of the voters in a referendum. Over the next months, "mundialization" spread quickly to other towns in France and Germany.

Mundialization is, essentially, a grass roots movement for world citizenship. The word is derived from the latin word for world — mundis. For a place to become "mundialized" means to become "worldly," to adopt a holistic worldview. It means social maturation, a process involving balance and coordination. Most declarations include the recognition of the right of citizens to extend their responsibilities beyond their regional or national boundaries, and a pledge to work for permanent world peace based on a system of just and enforceable world law.

The Charter is a basic declaration of the community's intentions to act as world territory. Among its basic provisions are the following:

- We declare that our security and welfare are linked to the security and welfare of all towns and districts of the world — these being like ourselves under the menace of totally destructive wars.
- We wish to work for peace with all towns and districts of the world and to cooperate with them so as to establish a world rule of law which will assure our common protection under the aegis of a democratically elected and controlled world federal authority.
- We request of our own government that funds be made available from the military budget and transferred to an international world fund usable for world elections.
- Without renouncing our attachment, duties and rights with respect to our own region and nation, we symbolically declare that our territory is world territory and as such is joined to the community of our whole world.
- We call on all towns and districts of the Earth to join us in this Charter of Solidarity.

As the French movement spread in late 1940s and 1950s, the same idea was simultaneously gaining ground in Japan. Still recovering from the Second World War and the first use of nuclear weapons, dozens of Japanese towns and cities began to adopt resolutions, linking the idea of world territory to global cooperation and peace.

Another related step was taken in Ellsworth, Maine. Along with the founding of World Government, a small piece of world territory was claimed; as a symbolic act, it signified that the entire planet is the home of humanity. In September, 1953, that dot of land in Ellsworth's Town Hall became World Citizen's Point.

Since the 50s, hundreds of places have declared themselves "mundialized," including Toronto, Bordeaux, Nimes, and various holy sites. By the late 1950s, the movement had reached major

Japanese cities such as Hiroshima, Nagasaki and Toyko. In the 1960s, Richfield, Ohio became America's first "world town," followed by Los Angeles, St. Louis, Minneapolis and Boston, among others.

The city of Dundas, Ontario, joined as the first mundialized Canandian community in June, 1967, at the same time initiating a worldwide "sister-city" movement. On behalf of the local Mundialization Committee, Hanna Newcombe had written to Kaga, Japan, suggesting that the two concepts be linked. In order to remind people of the significance of the step, she suggested three related actions at the local level when a community chose to mundialize:

- flying the UN flag beside the national flag in public places
- collecting a voluntary tax for UN activities
- twinning with another community that had mundialized

With the UN Secretary-General in attendance, Ottawa became a World City in 1970. Within three years more than a dozen other Canadian communities had joined the movement. The movement has continued to grow. In 1989, more than 30 mundialized communities across Canada were pursuing various sister-city and world peace projects. In the United States, four state governments — Minnesota, Wisconsin, Iowa and Illinois — have made declarations of world citizenship, and many more towns and cities have adapted the basic idea of mundialization to their own circumstances and cultures. Each place, in essence, has declared its solidarity with the rest of the world, recognizing that common interests and concerns unite humanity across artificial frontiers.

In Minnesota, the first state to adopt a declaration[†] in 1971, the governor and state legislature endorsed the idea. In Illinois and Iowa, the governor issued executive orders. In all cases, world citizenship was described as the only way to meet the common needs of humanity. Since then, dozens of civic, religious and political organizations have issued similar declarations.

As of 1988, there were about 1,000 mundialized places around the world. The list includes communities in at least 15 U.S. states, countless towns and cities across France and Japan, and com-

---

[†]See appendix.

munities in Italy, Germany, Belgium and India. Although it remains fundamentally a symbolic gesture, it also often involves cultural exchanges, an annual event to commemorate the decision or support the UN, voluntary UN contributions, and flying either a UN or world flag.

The world flag, which was first displayed at the founding of World Government in 1953, presents a human figure against a green-bordered globe. The symbolism is obvious: humanity encompasses the world, and both are bound to nature. It has been displayed at ceremonies in India, Jerusalem and during the fall of the Berlin Wall.

Implemented in conjunction with mundialization, "twinning" with a sister-city stresses the concept and practice of international cooperation. Sister-city activities of "twinned" and mundialized communities include:

- exchanging correspondence, students, teachers, or performers
- group visits

World Citizen Robin Lloyd raises World Flag at Berlin Wall.

- exhibits
- language classes
- material aid
- cultural festivals
- special school curricula
- commemorative projects such as parks or sculptures
- ecological projects such as tree planting and community gardens
- economic agreements.

Efforts like these both enhance knowledge of the world and improve international relations, overcoming the pervasive social conditioning that leads many people to view others as "aliens" or "enemies." Although such World Government programs may sometimes be met with opposition, this often provides an opportunity for public dialogue about the need for an alternative to the anarchy of nationalism. Each community that makes its declaration helps to extend an atmosphere in which global cooperation replaces force as the way to resolve the world's complex problems.

This may read like some utopian fantasy, a dream that cannot possibly be realized on our divided planet. Yet under the surface of nation-state mythology, a new and broader worldview is growing, despite the efforts of governments and multinational elites to smother it. Slowly, but inexorably, shared organic images are leading us to reorganize human society along holistic and harmonious lines. In less than three centuries we have produced technologies that have transformed the planet. They have united us into one, interdependent world. Now they can either liberate us or destroy us, depending upon our vision and wisdom.

Domination, whether of nature or other human beings, has become suicidal. In our new "global village," ownership must inevitably give way to partnership and unity. The choice is clear: humanity and its "territory" must live together in freedom or die.

Chapter 27

Economics: Toward Mutual Affluence

The linkages betweeen the geo-political instability of the nation-state system and global economic problems have finally become too visible even for politicians to ignore. These days our leaders speak grandly, though also mystically and often inconsistently, of an "interdependent world economic order." Their basic approach, however, precludes any realistic action to create or regulate this "order." Backed to the wall, mainstream economists generally agree that only draconian and wholesale measures can avert an inevitable worldwide crisis. Still, they hold fast to antiquated, cruel, obtuse or even whimsical solutions that ignore both political logic and moral imperatives.

In the meantime, multinational business entities manipulate the resources, accounting systems, revenues and even the governments of numerous nations with diverse currencies. Of the world's 100 largest economic units, almost half are corporations. The annual sales volume of General Motors is larger than the gross national product of 130 developing states. Able to subvert law and circumvent most government controls, the corporate "state" has become the most powerful tool for private profit — at public expense — ever devised.

Belately, lawmakers in the United States and elsewhere have begun to ask: Has concentrated economic power extended its reach so far that no government can stop it? Or does the scale and nature of world economics leave no alternative to these giant conglomerates? According to Ralph Nader, the "sovereignty of the consumer" is the most crucial aspect of this equation, as well as the ultimate countervailing force:

"Irresponsibility toward public interests becomes institutionalized whenever the making of decisions is so estranged from any
accountability for their discernable consequences.... The modern corporation is the engine of the world's largest production
machine. If it is to be more than a mindless, parochial jugger-
naut, the hands of diverse values and trusteeships for future
generations must be exerted on the steering wheel. There
should no longer be victims without representation. In any just
legal system a victim would have the right to decide with others
the behavior of the perpetrator and his recompense."

According to one United Nations report, although multinationals are often depicted as instruments of human welfare, many
people view them as dangerous agents of imperialism. Admitting
its own impotence to control them, the UN has concluded that
multinationals are "not subject to control and regulations by a
single authority which can aim at ensnaring a maximum degree of
harmony between their operations and the public interest." In
other words, they are out of control. Can this be changed? Can
multinationals be made accountable? Can economic power be
diffused, reducing the gap between the owners of corporate
equity — the haves, and the have-nots — the other 95 percent of
humanity?

According to the *Universal Declaration of Human Rights*,
everyone has a right to a decent standard of living — to food,
clothing, medical care, housing, social services, and security
against unemployment, sickness, disability, widowhood, and
old age (art. 25). Each of us also has the right to own property,
alone or in association with others (art. 17).

But what is property? Is it merely a home, a car, a TV and
some clothes? Or does it involve a set of related rights? If a few
individuals "own" most industrial capital and everyone else
"owns" little or nothing, income becomes grossly distorted and
inevitably the process of supply and demand breaks down. Thus,
in law, property involves rights as well as material objects, the
powers and privileges a person enjoys in his relationship to
things. According to Norman Kurland, director of the Center for
Economic and Social Justice, choosing and using particular
things to meet one's needs is the link between the individual and
social power. Since power — the means to influence change —
exists whether or not particular people own property, anyone

concerned about multinationals must keep in mind, as Daniel Webster put it, that "power naturally and inevitably follows the ownership of property."

Despite this warning, no industrial nation has yet adopted a democratic ownership strategy. Instead, national economic policies and institutions permit massive amounts of productive capital to be "owned" by a small minority. While this minority receives income far in excess of their need or capacity, the majority are left with unmet needs and inadequate purchasing power. Outmoded capital investment financing methods — using mainly the accumulated savings of individuals or their corporations — bring massive amounts of capital into existence without creating new owners. This guarantees that broad ownership will not be achieved. It also weakens the market mechanism, since it limits purchasing power for the majority. Finally, it prevents the development of general affluence, the only humane goal for a democratic economy. To compensate, many nations have empowered "big government" to protect the property-less many. But whenever political and economic power is combined in the hands of an elitist government, whether it calls itself "socialist" or "democratic," the prospects for individual freedom grow dimmer. Relying on "big government" to protect us from corporate oppression is like seeking justice from the accomplice of someone who has robbed you. Nader calls the dynamic an "institutionalized fusion of corporate desires with public bureaucracy." Whatever you call it, the result is that the economic policies of "big government" are hardly likely to foster widespread ownership of capital.

Another suggested panacea is "full employment." But without redistribution of the wealth or income produced by capital, most of the fully employed will not have sufficient purchasing power. If the goal of the economic system is to provide affluence instead of busywork and "equal poverty," full employment will not be sufficient. It may actually be a social hazard. Aspiring to restore a pre-industrial state of toil that modern technology once promised to make obsolete, full employment is actually an unnatural policy which cannot be enforced without ultimately demoralizing or even destroying the economy's productive sector.

The myopic economic policies of virtually all nations have, in short, contributed materially to a wide range of both social and economic dilemmas. Concentration of capital ownership has escalated, along with class and group conflict and violence. Crimes against property have increased. Alienation is widespread among the young, workers, minority groups, and the disadvantaged. Workers express fear and resistance to new technologies, making it more difficult to fully exploit the technological potential for improving the lives of the general public. Organized labor presses for increased income through wages, a self-defeating demand, rather than through ownership of industry. Growing dependency on "big government" strips the autonomy of local government, small business and the academic community. Rational planning for economic well-being, as well as for a more livable and humane environment, becomes virtually impossible.

This catalog of woes, added to the previously described problems of the nation-state, suggests several conclusions. Perhaps the most fundamental of these is that economic opportunity must be viewed as not merely the opportunity to work but to own capital — to acquire it without having to invade the property of others or reduce one's already inadequate consumption. In addition:

- Individual liberties and a democratic form of government cannot exist unless every person has the means to become a "have" rather than a "have not."
- The nation-state, as an economic institution, has been overtaken by industry and technology in general and by the rise of the multinational conglomerates in particular.
- While producing goods and services in sufficient, and sometimes excess, quantities to meet general needs, multinationals have no equitable distributive philosophy or system through which workers can benefit directly from ownership of the world's productive forces.
- Neither socialism nor capitalism can meet both the material and spiritual needs of humanity as a species or as free individuals.
- The elimination of armaments from the national economic scene would result in the raising of living standards worldwide, with social, cultural and spiritual benefits beyond measure.
- A distributive economy based on democratic ownership of

the means of production, emphasizing affluence while protecting the values of freedom, equality and justice, is essential not only to long-term economic stability but to survival itself.

In other words, ownership of tools and economic institutions must be handled globally, and every individual has a right to a share.

Democratic Ownership

To claim world citizenship is to claim partnership with planet Earth. But this claim also implies possession of one's rightful home and all it contains. Just as no one chooses his or her parents or place of birth, no one can rationally justify exclusive ownership of resources needed by everyone — the atmosphere, oceans, soil, water, even the sun. These are common to the human species.

Before establishing ownership as our heritage, however, we must first assert global citizenship. National citizenship perpetuates the philosophy of economic scarcity; world citizenship, in contrast, is the corollary of Earth ownership. Unless the individual assumes true ownership of the world, false owners are likely to destroy it. The world's problems, one UN secretary-general has said, are "beyond the control of any group of nations." Prospects are deteriorating rapidly for improved relations between industrialized and developing countries. As evidenced recently in the Soviet Union, economic decline can and will cause the disintegration of entire societies.

Until the emergence of World Government, no single organization had translated humanity's theoretical ownership of the Earth into practical ownership for the individual and humankind. Nation-states, of course, still oppose the idea. Either they are sovereign, or humanity. Either national law is paramount, or world law. Meanwhile, multinationals are nearing total "ownership." If they succeed, the inevitable result will be a violent world conflict between the "have-nots" and the 5 percent holding shares in the Total Corporation.

There is an alternative: direct participation in the profits of the entire industrial machinery of the world. The only way to eliminate poverty is to provide everyone with sufficient assets to achieve affluence. Such a global Mutual Affluence System is the philosophical basis of World Government economics.

If everyone is to have a chance to own a share of capital, however, the current automatic flow of most newly formed capital into the hands of the upper 5 percent will have to stop. Lacking capital, credit or political power, most workers are helpless to change their basic economic circumstances. Even if a worker joins a union, this group is not likely to demand more purchasing power through capital ownership for less work. If, however, the worker also asserts his other identities — consumer, tax-payer, and citizen, his power increases. The growth of mutual and money market funds are highly instructive in this regard; they suggest the possibility of creating a worker/consumer global mutual fund to share a piece of the world action. Such a fund could turn workers into investors.

There is, however, another missing link, the one element that is essential to the development of "mutual affluence," the lubricant without which no plan can work — a world currency.

World Money

But first, what is money? Obviously, without exchange value, coin or paper is worthless. The essential ingredient is trust and confidence. Whether the medium of exchange is shark's teeth, clay disks or gold bullion, the objects would be strictly ornamental without trust and confidence in their exchange value in the marketplace. The idea is that you can accept a dollar, kroner, franc, mark, ruble, rupee, yen or cedi and confidently pass it on in exchange for commensurate value. When trust is gone — for example, if the bank discovers that your money is actually forged — so is the exchange value. Trust is what allows the money to pass from hand to hand, buying bread and toothpaste and paying the rent.

When nations distrust one another, confidence in the value of their respective currencies declines. When the exchange of money itself becomes big business, the province of parasites who reap profits at public expense, distrust is institutionalized. Of course, a profit can be made from monetary distrust, as most central banks, speculators and multinationals know only too well. But in order to win in this game, someone must lose — those who naively believe their currency is a reliable "medium of exchange."

Today most people are painfully aware that most national currencies are unstable and unreliable. Their money no longer serves their interests as a constant, trustworthy means of exchange. In the 1970s the U.S. dollar was devalued twice in three years due to national deficits and the cost of foreign wars. During the late 1980s, the value of a U.S. dollar in relation to other "hard" currencies dropped by 50 percent. For most people, money has truly become the "root of evil " — that is, the means by which the rich exploit the poor.

Our confidence in money as a reliable medium of exchange for goods and services can only be reestablished on the world level. Only globally can problems of exchange of goods, equitable distribution of wealth-producing capital, and massive poverty be solved. This requires the development of global institutions. Further, it means that nation-states must give up the power to issue and control money. Multinational corporations are already moving in this direction. They shy away from identification with any one country, develop "indigenous" subsidiaries everywhere, create global management and decision-making structures, and allocate corporate resources on a world scale. But corporations are not designed to distribute wealth or resources equitably, or contribute to general affluence.

The use of World Money as a medium of exchange, in contrast, rests on a fundamental redefinition of wealth. As Buckminster Fuller once explained, we must have "an eternal world-around accounting which includes all generations to come, and which is consistent with the cosmic accounting of an eternally regenerative physical universal system." Under this system, humanity's "know how" would eventually make the scarcity model of economics obsolete. World accounting would also mean the right to ownership of the means to wealth.

A tentative move in the direction of World Money was the announcement in 1967 of a new "reserve asset," an "international" currency to supplement gold. Called "Special Drawing Rights" (SDRs), it began as a unit of credit based on the then-official value of gold. After being issued, however, SDRs could not be reconverted into gold. In other words, the central banks of the ten most developed nations, through the mechanism of the International Monetary Fund (IMF), created a new legal tender in order to increase liquidity between States. No single government sanctioned this creation.

Some economists hailed the development, suggesting that such collective action provided a way to counter the currency problems created by business speculation. Others, such as Adam Smith, argued that SDRs merely postponed a real solution. Though SDRs are a significant precedent, they are not a true step toward a world currency. They merely supplement the existing State-oriented economic system, and do nothing to alleviate the basic inequities.

When going abroad, travelers are urgently advised to convert their ready cash into traveler's checks, which are easily replaceable if lost. BankAmerica, one of the largest banks in the world, has advertised its checks as "world money." Backed by a negotiable currency, they are literally a medium of exchange for goods and services worldwide. This public service suggests a way in which a true form of world money, a global medium of exchange, can come about. Just as SDRs are recognized as legal tender between nations, world money can be established as legal tender between world citizens. The difference is that SDRs merely reinforce the economic competition or nations, while world money is designed to supply liquidity for the Mutual Affluence System. With intrinsic value as a global medium of exchange, it can be backed by today's "negotiable" currency and distributed by a legally-established bank.

At this point, World Money is actually circulating in the form of a $10 bill, issued by the World Government Treasury Account in the Riggs National Bank. As more World Money begins to circulate, however, the possibilities for business and personal exchange will increase.

Economic Rights

While consumers do exercise a limited form of "economic democracy" by using their money in the marketplace, their vote is indirect and certainly not a controlling factor. A true economic vote would be binding on the entire apparatus of production. Indeed, if we are to become "economic" citizens, our vote must be able to determine our personal and general economic conditions.

For example, a worker with one share in a particular multinational corporation has a limited, international economic vote. If the same person were to purchase a share in another corporation, his voting power would increase horizontally. The more corporations in which he owned shares, the broader his voting power. This is the basic principle of the mutual fund.

If a person owned shares in all multinational corporations, however, he would be something more than an international economic citizen; he would have become an international economic legislator. Theoretically, he could introduce a resolution at the yearly stockholders' meeting of every corporation in the world. At each, he could introduce the same resolution or policy idea. The cumulative effect of his actions would greatly magnify his limited voting power in the various businesses. Let's take the example one step further. Since shares in even a multinational are vulnerable in a volatile world, the international economic citizen needs some protection of his productive tools. Who or what can represent his long-term interests? A democratically-elected, global economic investment corporation. Such a World Citizens Investors' Corporation, feeding back profits to investors and holding their proxies, does not yet exist. But Employee Stock Ownership Plans (ESOPs) are small-scale attempts to upgrade the ownership stakes of workers. Other proposals, such as direct civic ownership of public transportation systems, utilities, and even giant corporations, have also been designed. The ultimate step is to include the general citizenry in ownership of the entire industrial pie.

Another necessary ingredient for the creation of general affluence is a new type of labor union, one designed to increase purchasing power through ownership of capital by workers and to promote design-science technology that decreases actual work time. Such a union of world citizens would also cross national frontiers, thus counteracting the ability of multinationals to bypass labor pressure in one country by moving production to another. Unions do not currently consider or defend the economic rights defined in Articles 17, 23 and 24 of the *Universal Declaration of Human Rights:*

- the right to own property and not to be deprived of it
- free choice of work under just and favorable conditions
- equal pay for equal work without any discrimination
- fair remuneration that provides a dignified existence, supplemented if necesssary by social protection
- rest and leisure, including reasonably limited work hours and periodic paid holidays

Most trade unions are still struggling to achieve international cooperation with workers' organizations in other countries where their multinational management have spread their tentacles. It will be some time before they develop both unity and a truly global viewpoint. Even then it is not likely to be more than a union-style UN, a federation of "sovereign unions" attempting, largely in vain, to negotiate with or govern multinationals. Separate unions cannot protect human economic rights; only a global organization, acting in the name of all worker/owners and transcending national boundaries, can overcome multinational power. In Article 20, the *Declaration of Human Rights* sanctions just such a global association; and Article 23(4) implies that it could take the form of a world-wide trade union.

***

In sum, the major elements required for the development of a Mutual Affluence System include:

- a world bank under the aegis of World Government
- a global currency system separate from national currencies
- a democratically controlled investment corporation through which securities in industries throughout the world can be purchased and voting equity can be exercised
- a world citizens labor union, aimed at employee stock ownership, increased purchasing power and decreased work time
- an institute of economic justice to educate people about this new global ownership approach, bring new economic thinking to leaders, and inform multinational managers about the

social, ecological, economic and moral advantages of this philosophy.

None of these proposals is impossible to implement. Certain trade unions, for instance, are leaning toward ESOPs as a way to avert a collision between "big business" and "big labor." The corporate call for "world peace through world trade" meanwhile indicates a recognition that war is a no-growth enterprise. The emergence of a united Europe in 1992 will have profound implications for global monetary policy, beginning with the attempt to develop a more stable currency system for what will be the world's largest economic entity. Taken together, however, the elements of a Mutual Affluence System can promise more: a global economic order, one capable of harnessing both the human energy and productive capacity that will be needed in order to transform the world, bringing the gifts of economic sufficiency and peace to all.

Chapter 28

The Practice of Freedom

"There is no first step to world government. World government is the first step."

— *Anatomy of Peace*, Emery Reves

I f we are going to save the world — that is, restore the biosphere and save ourselves as a species — we will have to develop and live by new rules. Only through the recognition and enforcement of world law can our basic rights be protected and the warmaking of the nation-states be stopped.

As I have stressed throughout this guide, individual action is the appropriate place to start. The assertion of human sovereignty is essential; in fact, it is the foundation of world citizenship. But individual gestures, even to the extent of putting your body on the border lines of the world, will not be enough. Ultimately, we will need a consensus of many individuals, a "commonweal" or body of citizens committed to the general welfare of the planet. At the collective level, world citizenship incorporates not only the needs and will of the individual human being, but also the will of humanity itself.

That word — humanity — is often used glibly. Everyone talks about saving humanity these days. But truly recognizing humanity as a being in itself, a whole greater than its parts, is a challenging step. One useful way to view it is that we live today in a post-natal period of humanity. It is young and still inexperienced, but it has been born. Humanity is a child with a nervous system, and all of us are dynamically connected to it.

This is a difficult realization, to be sure. And mostly we have negative evidence. Almost every day we are told that humanity is in danger. Well, if it's true, hadn't we better extend the reach of law to protect this child? In other words, isn't it time to "legalize" humanity?

As we approach the year 2000, a window of historic opportunity is opening. For more than 40 years, world citizenship has been an evolving agreement between individuals to act in a civilized way on the global level. Now, as the system of nation-states forged in the 18th Century is near breakdown, we can take concrete steps toward a higher level of political coherence. What we need next is a constitutional framework, a structure that fully acknowledges individual sovereignty and simultaneously makes one world of peace possible. Today millions of ordinary people think of themselves as citizens of the world. At least a million of them have formally declared their global allegiance. But this clearly hasn't been enough. Abuses of human rights continue in most parts of the nationalistic world. Dictatorships still flourish. The arms race has spread from the developed to the developing countries. While starvation persists, war budgets skyrocket. Pollution has become endemic.

Something fundamental to the process of creating a peaceful and healthy planet is still lacking. For stateless people and others "outside" the nation-state system, World Government is a useful and logical first step. But in our anarchic world, torn by terrorism and threatened daily by the nuclear "option," issuing documents and proving legal points is not enough. We are at a turning point: either humanity becomes legitimate or the dysfunctional nation-state system will eliminate it.

Planetery Process

Around the world there are thousands of peace organizations and countless allied organizations, at least a thousand "world communities" and a million world citizens. The missing ingredient, however, is an organizational bridge between global activists — both "first world" peace-workers and "third world" refugees, and the broader public which embraces the same goals but so far hesitates to make an active commitment.

That bridge, I suggest, is a constitutional framework. To become a living document, a world constitution will have to incorporate both the changing and the eternal elements of human society. It will have to reflect the experience of the past and the innovations of the present. Hopefully it will define a rapidly-changing world that is advancing toward the fourth level of dynamic identification — holism. Finally, it will have to reflect humanity — as sovereign individuals, as members of specific societies, and as a species, maturing in wisdom and loving communion. Not a simple task. Once created, this constitution must also be adopted by world society. Thus, planning for a world constitutional convention cannot wait until the last minute. When the time comes, the constituency must already be organized.

In November, 1989, that revolutionary process began with an initial planning conference in Toronto, Canada. Guided by the renowned cybernetician Stafford Beer, a group of World Citizens envisioned a ten-year process that will culminate in the worldwide acceptance of world law. According to Beer, president of the World Organization of General Systems and Cybernetics, this process of peacemaking has been immeasureably aided by the web of communication he calls the "technosphere."

The world of rock — the geosphere, is surrounded by the biosphere, and it in turn is now enrobed by the technosphere. The existence of the technosphere makes it possible for people to "meet" without being physically, geographically or politically in one place. A group of thirty people, an "Infoset," can share information and turn their insights into action, transcending the outmoded classifications of country, economic bloc or race. Once a small number of Infosets have been formally established, this mode of human collaboration will breed naturally. Before long the technosphere will be full of self-organizing mini-parliaments. In addition, selected World Citizens in mundialized world communities will be linked by satellite conferencing to address global concerns such as war and environmental devastation. For years, Beer has been testing the process through which Infosets identify and select the issues they will address. More recently he has developed a procedure, called Team Tensegrity, that organizes the Infoset as a non-hierarchical democracy and then coordinates various Infosets, thirty at a time. His mathematically-based design embodies the structural strength (tensegrity) of the geodesic dome invented by world-class thinker Buckminster Fuller and translates it into human terms. Old tools are no longer sufficient to meet the "macro" challenges of our time. They usually limit action rather than facilitate it. But through cybernetics, the science of effective organization, World Government will be able to develop and coordinate new designs for peace. The old world, characterized by the need to manage "things," is vanishing, Beer has explained. In the new world, the greatest need is to manage "complexity." Through cybernetic processes, world citizens can now take on this management challenge and ultimately achieve the horizontal reorganization of the planet.

Over the coming years, numerous Infosets will be organized. Each mini-convention will start without a pre-conceived ideological agenda. The only common denominator will be the identity of participants — World Citizens. Each person in an Infoset will receive a manual outlining both the individual meeting and long-term process.

Points of Entry

The road is long, and the time is short. After more than four decades as a World Citizen, I will not underestimate either the task or the opposition. Despite every warning signs, nations cling to their obsolete, arbitrary definitions and destructive tactics. But after all these years, I also cannot ignore or minimize the power of the individual or of the ideas that have grown from the courageous actions of World Citizens everywhere.

And so, if you agree that the nation-state is the problem and that world law is the solution, if you want to reclaim your sovereignty and assert your human rights, what can you do?

1. Declare your World Citizenship, of course. Study the idea, its implications and responsibilities. Try it out — by obtaining and using world documents that meet your personal needs. When you cross a border, show your World Passport, even if it is only a "back-up" document at first. Confront and question bureaucratic authority wherever you meet it. In short, become an active player in the "game" of creating a truly free world.

2. Don't hestitate to utilize that newsletter of the technosphere — the mass media. When you engage in any public action, you are both exercising sovereignty and educating the public. Putting your body on the line, as it were, you become a "happening." And that's news. But this also imposes major responsibilities. First, you must identify yourself, both politically and visually, so that the public knows who has taken the action and why. Tell the media people who you are, why you are doing what you are doing, and when. Provide whatever background material you have to justify your actions and explain your motives.

To identify yourself "visually" may mean using signs, posters, flags and, yes, even uniforms. Remember that Gandhi dressed all his civil disobedience rebels in white khadi clothes and caps. Uniforms connote both authority and public service. When you take action in a public cause, you are acting both with authority — sovereignty — and in a spirit of public service, much like a postman, nurse or policeman. Also keep in mind that you are, unfortunately, in competition with every other action taking place at the same time. While the media are ubiquitous, they are not everywhere at once.

Reporters and cameramen are assigned on a daily basis by their assignment editors. Give them sufficient time before your event to consider whether they want to cover it. Another important consideration is that the media work on three levels: local, national and international. Most newspapers and all wire services have assignments editors relating to all three levels. Make sure to direct your press release to the editor handling the level on which you want your story to appear. Assignment editors will nevertheless often decide on what level to use your story, depending on its significance. Given the global nature of mass communication, even if only one wire service reporter files a story, it can be read by millions of people the next day. In Berne, for example, I once called a press conference, and hired a small theater in a famous restaurant. No one showed up except a single television crew. "What are you going to do, Garry?" the newsman asked me. "I'm going to give the conference to the empty seats," I replied. "Great," he said. That night the 7 o'clock national TV news carried my address about world citizenship to 200 empty seats.

Never but never complain to the press if they, 1) didn't use your story, 2) used it, but not as you hoped, or 3) characterized you as a "crackpot," "illusionary," "radical," etc. As long as they spell your name right, be happy. "Name recognition" is half the battle. Don't give up. Your continued commitment will carry weight with the press. For years, I was characterized as a "self-styled world citizen," as if I was some egomaniac. Sometimes I would reply that Socrates was also "self-styled." Be both hard-nosed and as innocent as a babe. The combination is dynamite.

A few more specifics may be helpful in your dealings with the media:

- Always write a press release before taking an action. In that way you can control, more or less, what goes into the story. Reporters also need your version as background for what they will write. Keep in mind, however, that you do not control the media. In a democratic society, freedom of the press is a given. Your papers for the press simply help the reporter do his or her job.

- Keep the release short, preferably one double-spaced page. Reporters are time stressed. Your first sentence must include WHO, WHAT, WHEN, WHERE, WHY and HOW. This can even be encapsulated in a headline, with a sub-head that clarifies the situation:

WORLD CITIZENS TO PUSH WORLD TERRITORY VOTE
Monday Action at City Council Stresses World Law

- Give the general release date in the upper left-hand corner, and a contact name and telephone number in the upper right-hand corner of your release. End it with — 30 —. That's a tradition.

- If you refer to other material in the release, note "appended" and include them as additions. This is also true for back-ground material or biographies.

- Releases can now be faxed to newspapers, wire services, radio and TV stations. But don't count on having them read. Everyone is doing it. Courier service is more efficient. Mail is fine if you have the time. But don't neglect to follow up with a telephone call to the assignment editor of your choice.

- When it's over, write a short note of thanks to a reporter who did a good job with your story. They are human, after all, and appreciate recognition. The same applies to an editor, if you are certain that he or she helped in the coverage of your activities.

■ Above all, don't be annoyed if your story does not make it into print. Your release can be used in many other ways — as a record of your activities, communique to other organizations or individuals, or as background for your next action.

3. If you have the time, the talents or the inclination, get into politics, preferably as part of the World Citizens party or by urging your community to become World Territory. You don't have to run for president. World issues are relevant at any level of government. The phrase "Think globally and act locally" should be amended to "Think globally and then act globally" because the global is also local. Seeking office allows you to put a platform for fundamental change before the public, translating basic ideas about human rights into concrete programs that match the community in which you are working. At the local and state levels, mundialization is a practical, multi- faceted program with important social and economic implications.

4. Use the existing international covenants and agreements mentioned in this book, particularly the *Universal Declaration of Human Rights,* whenever and wherever you can. Get to know their history and appreciate their potential power.

5. If you are fed up with supporting war through your taxes, you will find support for an alternative in both the Universal Declaration and Nuremberg Principles. In recognizing individual sovereignty, the Declaration provides a legal defense for non-payment of war taxes. For U.S. citizens, additional case law, such as *Filartiga v. Pena-Irala* (630 F.2nd, 2nd Cir, 1980) and *Paquette Habana* (175 U.S. 677, 700, 1900) provides supplementary legal arguments for local tax authorities. The main justification for national tax refusal is your desire, as a World Citizen, to eliminate war. But you also have an inalienable right to choose your political allegiance and support it. Like choosing this allegiance, paying taxes is voluntary. You can thus plausibly argue that

voluntary payment of taxes to World Government rather than to a national government is essential to your security, freedom and well-being. Rather than funding the military, then, you can fund the evolution of World Government by fowarding the military portion of your tax bill to the bank account established for that purpose: World Government Treasury Dept., Riggs National Bank, Washington, D.C.

As a World Citizen, you can receive an Annual Return Form, which provides various alternatives for the peace-oriented use of your tax payments. When you return it to the World Government Treasury Department with your payment, you will receive a receipt which you can photocopy and forward to your national tax office, along with the remainder of your tax. The World Service Authority will also supply a letter explaining your action, and back you up if the need arises. Your payments to World Government will make it possible to assist refugees, develop a World Mutual Abundance Bank, and develop both our constitution and a global economic system based on general affluence.

6. Whatever you decide to do, keep in touch. Unlike national government, World Government really wants your feedback as much as your money. And it doesn't demand obedience, or ask that you give anything up. If your human rights are violated, the World Service Authority will take your case to the highest level. As the record shows, when the interests of humanity and the whims of a nation-state collide, humanity CAN win.

So, don't forget to write or phone:

World Service Authority
1012 14th Street NW
Washington, DC 20005 — U.S.A
Telephone: 202-638-2662
Fax: 202 638-0638

or

Hills Nakano #208
1-1-12 Nogata, Nakano-ku
Tokyo 165, Japan
Telephone (03) 319-5170
Fax: (03) 319-5127

And finally, as I said on the day that World Government was founded, "Do not be indifferent to your own survival and happiness. Examine these ideas and words with the searing blade of your own conscience and reason. They will stand even then. And do not hesitate for lack of experience. This work is unprecedented in these modern times. Thus we are all youths in this task. But experience can only be gained by living our goal from the outset, by being members of the world community. And if we stumble, falter, even fall, there are others to carry on, for the reality of humanity's unity is a truth that cannot die."

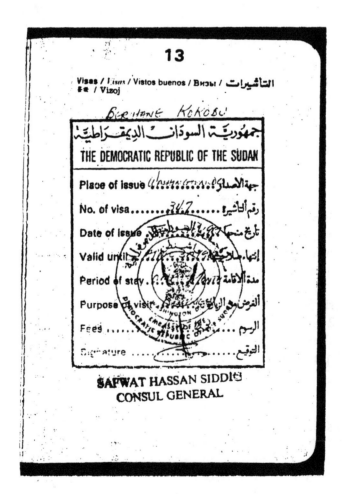

Pledge of Allegiance

I do hereby, willingly and consciously, declare myself to be a Citizen of the World. As a World Citizen, I pledge my planetary civic commitment to World Government, founded on three universal principles of One Absolute Value, One World and One Humanity which constitute the basis of World Law. As a World Citizen I acknowledge the World Government as having the right and duty to represent me in all that concerns fundamental human rights and the General Good of humankind and the Good of All.

As a Citizen of World Government, I affirm my awareness of my inherent responsibilities and rights as a legitimate member of the total world community of all men, women and children, and will endeavor to fulfill and practice these whenever and wherever the opportunity presents itself.

As a Citizen of World Government, I recognize and re-affirm citizenship loyalties and responsibilities within the communal, state and/or national grouping consistent with the principles of unity above which constitute now my planetary civic commitment.

EPILOG

A Borderless World Order

Since the opening of Eastern Europe and the latest war in the Persian Gulf we have been hearing and reading about a "new world order." In the foregoing pages, as in my two previous books, I have tried to articulate the reality of a self-evident and existing — if politically unacknowledged — world order. According to President George Bush, who began using the phrase shortly after allied forces launched the most massive military campaign since World War II, it would be "a world where the rule of law, not the rule of the jungle, governs the conduct of nations." Bush didn't — and indeed couldn't — elaborate on the modus operandi. "I'm not talking here," he explained on April 13, 1991 in Montgomery, Alabama, "of a blueprint that will govern the conduct of nations or some supernatural structure or institution." Instead, the implied promise was that through the benign use of continued national power by armed states a democratic revolution would transform the world. Dictators would fall or be broken, and the use of force would be replaced by peaceful dialogue between reasonable men and women.

Thus, despite the "rule of law," what still prevailed in Bush's vision of a "new world order" was jungle law, with the U.S. president as de facto "king."

Rhetoric and reality are, of course, poles apart. The truth is that the U.S.-led effort to impose "order" on the world is neither new nor benign. Like every plan grounded in nationalism that has preceeded it, this 1990s version is not only fundamentally flawed but mortal to Earth and its many species.

Given the hoary dictum that like begets like, or in socio-political terms, that violence begets violence, in the euphoric aftermath of the war to "liberate" Kuwait several hundred thousand Kurdish refugees faced death and starvation for taking the U.S. President at his word, and hellish fires blanketed the Middle East sky with the black soot of hundreds of oil fires, a prophetic warning that nature will not abide our earthly follies. Meanwhile, despite the "end" of the Cold War, the race to create new and "smarter" weapons, and sell them to countries unable to feed their poor, continued without pause. Millions faced starvation or disease in Africa and Bangladesh. Simultaneously, the decline of Soviet power and upheavals in Central Europe set loose a wave of ethnic and nationalist rivalries destined to create new and more dangerous disorder in the prevailing world anarchy.

Even if we take the intentions of those who talk of a "new world order" at face value — a dangerous exercise of blind faith in itself — it is obvious that good intentions are not enough. Despite the failure of the United Nations to make peace, the Bush Doctrine, like Wilson's utopian plan to "make the world safe for democracy" by assembling a "league of nations," rests on the illusory premise that influential leaders and exclusive sovereign nations can agree to run the planet in a reasonable way. This is more necessary than ever, the leaders of the nuclear "superpowers" say, due to the ever-growing ecological threats faced by the world. Such an idea, however, is based on a form of global imperialism — fewer nations making the critical decisions, and an even bigger gap between the leaders and the led, the powerful and the powerless. It also leaves humanity itself out of the equation.

Bush's "new world order" was actually designed by Richard Nixon and Henry Kissinger. Their idea, embraced by their protege Gerald Ford, echoed by Jimmy Carter, and secretly pursued by both Reagan and Bush, is that existing centers of industrial and military power — the United States, Japan, Western Europe, the Soviet Union and China — will "administer" — a "stable" system of world order for the indefinite future. To these global executives, "administer" is a synonym for military command. Under this contemptible and debased arrangement, the dominant actors work out the terms of cooperation and limited competition, based on the economic and political status quo. But "order and stability are not always found in the status quo," political commentator William Safire has noted. "When the tectonic plates underlying nation-states begin to move, we heighten the pressure by failing to recognize new realities." This imperial design places little or no emphasis on social and economic justice, human rights or global civic rights; on the contrary, justice and human rights are often considered obstacles to the notion of planetary "order" and therefore must be sacrificed when and wherever they conflict with the smooth functioning of an ultra-nationalistic bureaucratic system. Despite this insidious attempt to centralize global political power along archaic nationalistic lines, however, the world of nations itself is clearly breaking apart. This 18th century horse-and-buggy political system, under the pressure of ethnic and religious rivalries, brutal economic competition, regional antagonisms and instantaneous communication, is in the advanced stages of disintegration. Poverty, violence and disease are accelerating worldwide crises that no imperial order can wish away. Unfortunately, the next "world order plan" — unless the world's people reject it — will probably be the most dangerous yet: planetary dictatorship by a small elite that tolerates no opposition. The response to demands for freedom and self-determination may very well be the imposition of a global police state.

This grim Orwellian scenario is forwarded with the conviction that there remains time to turn the tide in a new dimensional direction; in other words, to transform politics in order to meet the immense challenges of the 21st century. The current vulnerability of the nation-state system offers humanity the opportunity to finally assert its own power and sovereignty.

This conclusion is not merely a case of wishful thinking; it is based on a lifetime of experience as a world citizen, as well as on recent encounters in the post Cold-War world. Since 1989, you see, we have been witnessing an historic groundswell of interest in a truly new world order based on the replacement of exclusive nation-states with a world government of free citizens. Though we may not have recognized it, we have glimpsed it in Europe, across Africa, and in Asia.

At the root, what ties the many popular movements across the planet into one whole is the universal imperative and popular call for a new global system. Even before the "new world order" was proclaimed by President Bush, I saw it at work in microcosm in Japan, where I spent several months in 1989 and 1990 developing a Pacific Rim base for the World Service Authority, as well as across Europe and in the dissolving Soviet Empire.

In February, 1989, upon arriving in Japan, I had announced myself to Emperor Akihito, who had fortuitously declared his era of reign "Hesei," or "Achievement of Peace." My intentions and status as a world citizen were thus quite clear. In the wake of the crackdown on the "democracy" movement in China, hundreds of Chinese students were flooding our new Tokyo office to declare themselves beyond the power of their despotic state. In addition, Japanese labor laws were making life hard for foreign workers labeled "illegal" for overstaying their tourist visas. Each arbitrary and repressive action of Asian governments was leading more people to the realization that world citizenship might hold the key to their survival and freedom. Since then thousands of world passports have been issued to Asians who have begun to understand that world law is not a question of creating utopia but rather of survival itself. Meanwhile, in Eastern Europe people were rebelling against outdated and oppressive political systems. The Soviet empire was starting to crumble. One by one, old regimes were falling. By February, 1990, I knew I had to see these world-shaking changes for myself. At the same time, I could test whether Eastern Europe had become fertile ground for world citizenship and world law. I was not disappointed. Both Romania and Czechoslovakia promptly issued visas on my world passport, followed later by Bulgaria, Cyprus, Peru, and Mexico. At the airport in East Berlin, TV cameras from WDR in Cologne recorded my first encounter with two local border officials. With people streaming through the East-West border station just minutes away, both men found it difficult to maintain the fiction of control. They let me through, recording the passport number on my transit visa. World citizenship had come to the New Europe.

On March 2, Czechoslavakian President Vaclav Havel expressed open support for world government when I presented his honorary World Passport. "Since I became president," he told me, "they took away my civilian passport, so I have no identity documents at present. This is the first I have received since becoming president. It is a most precious document." In an interview in Vilnius with Vytautis Landsbergis, president of the newly-declared Lithuanian republic, I suggested that the Baltic states immediately declare themselves "world states," taking advantage of the process of political fission overtaking the world. "Independence first," President Landsbergis replied, "then world citizenship." Moscow Mayor Gavril Popov was also supportive when he received his honorary passport on April 23, joining the Lithuanian President and mayors in U.S., European and Japanese cities who have acknowledged the "mundialist" movement. I entered Japan again at Narita Airport without incident — or visa — and proceeded to issue honorary world passports to the Emperor himself, Toyko's Governor Shunichi Suzuki, Prime Minister Toshiki Kaifu — who advocated a "new world order" in every speech — and Andrei Sakharov, who was visiting for a Nobel Laureates' forum.

The Toyko office was bustling. Over 2000 people, mostly Southeast Asians, had so far requested world citizen registration, passports, birth certificates and political asylum cards. After an article appeared in *Asia Magazine,* a widely read Pacific Rim weekly, inquiries also came in from Hong Kong, Singapore, Malaysia, Thailand, Taiwan and Indonesia. During this period, up to 300 letters a day were arriving at our Washington, D.C. office.

But old ideas die hard, and nation-states do not surrender their authority without a struggle. Thus, I was only mildly surprised when five officials of the Japanese Immigration Service arrived at my office on July 16, 1990 with an order for my "deportation." For the next two weeks I was held in a Toyko Immigration jail, along with Pakistanis, Bangladeshis, Sri Lankans, Burmese, Filippinos, Chinese and Vietnamese, all scheduled for deportation.

Finally, the word came down — not from the Japanese government but instead from the U.S. State Department. In collusion with the Immigration and Naturalization Service, the State Department had decided arbitrarily to label me now an "indefinite parolee in the public interest." In doing so, U.S. officials had blithely annulled the former "excludable alien" classification that had followed me since May, 1977, when the INS refused to let me enter the country at Dulles Airport.

The Japanese released me without charge and provided a paddy wagon ride out to Narita. I returned to the United States — while WSA Tokyo continued full blast — unconcerned about the arbitrary label of the State Department and INS. Arriving in Los Angeles, I simply presented my World Passport to a bored

Immigration officer, who glanced at it curiously. I was admitted and moved on.

And the moral of the story? Each time someone says no to the nation-state system or places him or herself outside its despotic jurisdiction, another "brick" is removed from the surreal wall. It is only a matter of time before humanity, in wisdom, love and peace, accepts the perenniel truth that all borders are fictitious. In truth, the "borderless world order" is already here. It begins with you and me, fellow human beings under the twinkling, gently mocking stars.

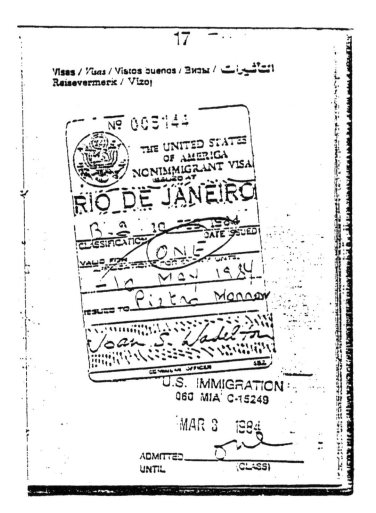

Appendices

World Government of World Citizens

Main Office

Suite 1106 Continental Building
1012 14th Street NW
Washington, DC 20005
(202) 638-2662; Fax (202) 638-0638

Administration

World Service Authority
Garry Davis, Founder
Ingrid von Teslon-Dennison, President

Judiciary

Dr. Francis Boyle, Coordinator

Commissions

Communications: Syd Cassid, Coordinator
Cultural: Sir Yehudi Menuhin, Coordinator;
    Katherine Dunham, Deputy
Cybernetics: Stafford Beer, Coordinator
Design-Science: William Perk, Coordinator
Economics: Harry Ball-Wilson, Coordinator
Education: Guru Nitya C. Yati, Coordinator
Environment: James Lovelock, Coordinator;
    Edward Goldsmith, Deputy
Forestry: Badi Lenz, Coordinator
Health: Michio Kushi, Coordinator
Ind. Cybernetics: Jurgen Ladewig, Coordinator
Ocean: E.R. Welles, Coordinator
Space: Isaac Asimov, Coordinator; Carol S. Rosin, Deputy
Women: Georgia Lloyd, Coordinator

World Government Treasury Department

Riggs National Bank
Acct. #1-262-73-4

List of Nation-states

Here is the complete list of the fictional political world of the 1990s. For instance, to realize its transitional character, compare it with the list of 1890s. What then will it be in the 2090s?

The asterisks indicate states that have honored the World Passport on a case-by case basis according to WSA records (see visas throughout the book).

Afghanistan*
Albania
Algeria*
Andorra
Angola*
Antigua*
Argentina*
Australia*
Austria*
Bahamas*
Bahrain*
Banglandesh*
Barbados*
Belau
Belgium*
Belize*
Benin*
Bhutan
Bolivia*
Botswana*
Brazil*
Brunei*
Bulgaria*
Burkina Faso*
Burma*
Burundi*
Cambodia*
Cameroon*
Canada*

Cape Verde*
Central African
    Republic
Chad*
Chile
China*
Columbia*
Congo*
Costa Rica*
Cuba*
Cyprus*
Czechoslovakia*
Denmark
Djibouti*
Dominica
Dominican
    Republic*
Ecuador*
Egypt*
El Salvador
Eq. Guinea*
Estonia
Ethiopia*
Fiji
Finland
France*
French Guiana*
French Polynesia*
Gabon

Gambia*
Germany*
Ghana*
Greece*
Grenada*
Guatemala*
Guinea*
Guinea-Bissau
Guyana*
Haiti*
Honduras*
Hong Kong*
Hungary*
Iceland*
India*
Indonesia
Iran
Iraq*
Ireland
Israel*
Italy*
Ivory Coast*
Jamaica*
Japan*
Jordan*
Kenya*
Kiribatti
Korea, North
Korea, South*

Kuwait
Laos*
Latvia*
Lebanon*
Lesotho
Liberia*
Libya
Lithuania*
Liechtenstein
Luxembourg*
Madagascar
Malawi*
Malaysia
Maldives
Mali*
Martinique*
Marshall Islands
Mauritania*
Mauritius*
Mexico*
Micronesia
Monoca
Mongolia
Morocco
Mozambique*
Namibia
Nauru
Nepal*
Netherlands
New Caledonia*
New Zealand*
Nicaragua*
Niger*
Nigeria*
Norway*
Oman
Pakistan*
Panama*
Papua New Guinea
Paraguay*
Peru*

Philippines*
Poland*
Portugal*
Qatar*
Romania*
Rwanda
St. Christopher
   & Nevis*
St. Marten
St. Vincent &
   the Grenadines*
St. Lucia
San Marino*
Sao Tome & Principe
Saudi Arabia*
Senegal*
Seychelles
Sierra Leone
Singapore
Solomon Islands
Somalia*
South Africa*
Spain*
Sri Lanka*
Sudan*
Suriname*
Swaziland
Sweden*
Switzerland*
Syria*
Taiwan*
Tanzania*
Thailand*
Togo*
Tonga
Trinidad & Tobago
Tunisia
Turkey*
Turks & Caicos
   Islands*
Tuvalu

Uganda
United
   Arab Emirates
United Kingdom
U.S.A.*
U.S.S.R.*
Uruguay
Vanuata*
Venda
Venezuala*
Vietnam
Virgin
   Islands (British)*
Western Samoa
Yemen (Arab
   Republic)*
Yugoslavia*
Zaire*
Zambia*
Zimbabwe*

UNIVERSAL DECLARATION OF HUMAN RIGHTS

PREAMBLE

Whereas recognition of the inherent dignity and of the equal and inalienable rights of all members of the human family is the foundation of freedom, justice and peace in the world,

Whereas disregard and contempt for human rights have resulted in barbarous acts which have outraged the conscience of mankind, and the advent of a world in which human beings shall enjoy freedom of speech and belief and freedom from fear and want has been proclaimed as the highest aspiration of the common people,

Whereas it is essential, if man is not to be compelled to have recourse, as a last resort, to rebellion against tyranny and oppression, that human rights should be protected by the rule of law,

Whereas it is essential to promote the development of friendly relations between nations,

Whereas the peoples of the United Nations have in the Charter reaffirmed their faith in fundamental human rights, in the dignity and worth of the human person and in the equal rights of men and women and have determined to promote social progress and better standards of life in larger freedom,

Whereas Member States have pledged themselves to achieve, in co-operation with the United Nations, the promotion of universal respect for and observance of human rights and fundamental freedoms,

Whereas a common understanding of these rights and freedoms is of the greatest importance for the full realization of this pledge,

2

Now, Therefore,

THE GENERAL ASSEMBLY

proclaims

THIS UNIVERSAL DECLARATION OF HUMAN RIGHTS as a common standard of achievement for all peoples and all nations, to the end that every individual and every organ of society, keeping this Declaration constantly in mind, shall strive by teaching and education to promote respect for these rights and freedoms and by progressive measures, national and international, to secure their universal and effective recognition and observance, both among the peoples of Member States themselves and among the peoples of territories under their jurisdiction.

Article 1. All human beings are born free and equal in dignity and rights. They are endowed with reason and conscience and should act towards one another in a spirit of brotherhood.

Article 2. Everyone is entitled to all the rights and freedoms set forth in this Declaration, without distinction of any kind, such as race, colour, sex, language, religion, political or other opinion, national or social origin, property, birth or other status.

Furthermore, no distinction shall be made on the basis of the political, jurisdictional or international status of the country or territory to which a person belongs, whether it be independent, trust, non-self-governing or under any other limitation of sovereignty.

Article 3. Everyone has the right to life, liberty and security of person.

Article 4. No one shall be held in slavery or servitude; slavery and the slave trade shall be prohibited in all their forms.

3

Article 5. No one shall be subjected to torture or to cruel, inhuman or degrading treatment or punishment

Article 6. Everyone has the right to recognition everywhere as a person before the law.

Article 7. All are equal before the law and are entitled without any discrimination to equal protection of the law. All are entitled to equal protection against any discrimination in violation of this Declaration and against any incitement to such discrimination.

Article 8. Everyone has the right to an effective remedy by the competent national tribunals for acts violating the fundamental rights granted him by the constitution or by law.

Article 9. No one shall be subjected to arbitrary arrest, detention or exile.

Article 10. Everyone is entitled in full equality to a fair and public hearing by an independent and impartial tribunal, in the determination of his rights and obligations and of any criminal charge against him.

Article 11. (1) Everyone charged with a penal offence has the right to be presumed innocent until proved guilty according to law in a public trial at which he has had all the guarantees necessary for his defence

(2) No one shall be held guilty of any penal offence on account of any act or omission which did not constitute a penal offence, under national or international law, at the time when it was committed. Nor shall a heavier penalty be imposed than the one that was applicable at the time the penal offence was committed

Article 12. No one shall be subjected to arbitrary interference with his privacy, family, home or correspondence, nor to attacks upon his hon-

4

our and reputation. Everyone has the right to the protection of the law against such interference or attacks.

Article 13. (1) Everyone has the right to freedom of movement and residence within the borders of each state.

(2) Everyone has the right to leave any country, including his own, and to return to his country.

Article 14. (1) Everyone has the right to seek and to enjoy in other countries asylum from persecution.

(2) This right may not be invoked in the case of prosecutions genuinely arising from non-political crimes or from acts contrary to the purposes and principles of the United Nations.

Article 15. (1) Everyone has the right to a nationality.

(2) No one shall be arbitrarily deprived of his nationality nor denied the right to change his nationality.

Article 16. (1) Men and women of full age, without any limitation due to race, nationality or religion, have the right to marry and to found a family. They are entitled to equal rights as to marriage, during marriage and at its dissolution.

(2) Marriage shall be entered into only with the free and full consent of the intending spouses.

(3) The family is the natural and fundamental group unit of society and is entitled to protection by society and the State.

Article 17. (1) Everyone has the right to own property alone as well as in association with others

(2) No one shall be arbitrarily deprived of his property.

Article 18. Everyone has the right to freedom of thought, conscience and religion; this right

5

nations, racial or religious groups, and shall further the activities of the United Nations for the maintenance of peace.

(3) Parents have a prior right to choose the kind of education that shall be given to their children.

Article 27. (1) Everyone has the right freely to participate in the cultural life of the community, to enjoy the arts and to share in scientific advancement and its benefits.

(2) Everyone has the right to the protection of the moral and material interests resulting from any scientific, literary or artistic production of which he is the author.

Article 28. Everyone is entitled to a social and international order in which the rights and freedoms set forth in this Declaration can be fully realized.

Article 29. (1) Everyone has duties to the community in which alone the free and full development of his personality is possible.

(2) In the exercise of his rights and freedoms, everyone shall be subject only to such limitations as are determined by law solely for the purpose of securing due recognition and respect for the rights and freedoms of others and of meeting the just requirements of morality, public order and the general welfare in a democratic society.

(3) These rights and freedoms may in no case be exercised contrary to the purposes and principles of the United Nations.

Article 30. Nothing in this Declaration may be interpreted as implying for any State, group or person any right to engage in any activity or to perform any act aimed at the destruction of any of the rights and freedoms set forth herein.

DPI/15 — September 1983 — 100M
Reprinted in U N, NY — 20126 — August 1988 — 100M

UNIVERSAL
DECLARATION
of
HUMAN RIGHTS

On december 10, 1948, the General Assembly of the United Nations adopted and proclaimed the Universal Declaration of Human Rights, the full text of which appears on the following pages. Following this historic act the Assembly called upon all Member countries to publicize the text of the Declaration and "to cause it to be disseminated, displayed, read and expounded principally in schools and other educational institutions without distinction based on the political status of countries or territories."

Final Authorized Text

UNITED NATIONS

OFFICE OF PUBLIC INFORMATION

includes freedom to change his religion or belief, and freedom, either alone or in community with others and in public or private, to manifest his religion or belief in teaching, practice, worship and observance.

Article 19. Everyone has the right to freedom of opinion and expression; this right includes freedom to hold opinions without interference and to seek, receive and impart information and ideas through any media and regardless of frontiers.

Article 20. (1) Everyone has the right to freedom of peaceful assembly and association.

(2) No one may be compelled to belong to an association.

Article 21. (1) Everyone has the right to take part in the government of his country, directly or through freely chosen representatives.

(2) Everyone has the right of equal access to public service in his country.

(3) The will of the people shall be the basis of the authority of government; this will shall be expressed in periodic and genuine elections which shall be by universal and equal suffrage and shall be held by secret vote or by equivalent free voting procedures.

Article 22. Everyone, as a member of society, has the right to social security and is entitled to realization, through national effort and international co-operation and in accordance with the organization and resources of each State, of the economic, social and cultural rights indispensable for his dignity and the free development of his personality.

Article 23. (1) Everyone has the right to work, to free choice of employment, to just and favourable conditions of work and to protection against unemployment.

(2) Everyone, without any discrimination, has the right to equal pay for equal work.

(3) Everyone who works has the right to just and favourable remuneration ensuring for himself and his family an existence worthy of human dignity, and supplemented, if necessary, by other means of social protection.

(4) Everyone has the right to form and to join trade unions for the protection of his interests.

Article 24. Everyone has the right to rest and leisure, including reasonable limitation of working hours and periodic holidays with pay.

Article 25. (1) Everyone has the right to a standard of living adequate for the health and well-being of himself and of his family, including food, clothing, housing and medical care and necessary social services, and the right to security in the event of unemployment, sickness, disability, widowhood, old age or other lack of livelihood in circumstances beyond his control.

(2) Motherhood and childhood are entitled to special care and assistance. All children, whether born in or out of wedlock, shall enjoy the same social protection.

Article 26. (1) Everyone has the right to education. Education shall be free, at least in the elementary and fundamental stages. Elementary education shall be compulsory. Technical and professional education shall be made generally available and higher education shall be equally accessible to all on the basis of merit.

(2) Education shall be directed to the full development of the human personality and to the strengthening of respect for human rights and fundamental freedoms. It shall promote understanding, tolerance and friendship among all

DECLARATION UNIVERSELLE DES DROITS DE L'HOMME

PRÉAMBULE

Considérant que la reconnaissance de la dignité inhérente à tous les membres de la famille humaine et de leurs droits égaux et inaliénables constitue le fondement de la liberté, de la justice et de la paix dans le monde,

Considérant que la méconnaissance et le mépris des droits de l'homme ont conduit à des actes de barbarie qui révoltent la conscience de l'humanité et que l'avènement d'un monde où les êtres humains seront libres de parler et de croire, libérés de la terreur et de la misère, a été proclamé comme la plus haute aspiration de l'homme,

Considérant qu'il est essentiel que les droits de l'homme soient protégés par un régime de droit pour que l'homme ne soit pas contraint, en suprême recours, à la révolte contre la tyrannie et l'oppression,

Considérant qu'il est essentiel d'encourager le développement de relations amicales entre nations,

Considérant que dans la Charte les peuples des Nations Unies ont proclamé à nouveau leur foi dans les droits fondamentaux de l'homme, dans la dignité et la valeur de la personne humaine, dans l'égalité des droits des hommes et des femmes, et qu'ils se sont déclarés résolus à favoriser le progrès social et à instaurer de meilleures conditions de vie dans une liberté plus grande,

Considérant que les États Membres se sont engagés à assurer, en coopération avec l'Organisation des Nations Unies, le respect universel et effectif des droits de l'homme et des libertés fondamentales,

Considérant qu'une conception commune de ces droits et libertés est de la plus haute importance pour remplir pleinement cet engagement,

— 2 —

L'ASSEMBLÉE GÉNÉRALE

proclame

LA PRÉSENTE DÉCLARATION UNIVERSELLE DES DROITS DE L'HOMME comme l'idéal commun à atteindre par tous les peuples et toutes les nations afin que tous les individus et tous les organes de la société, ayant cette Déclaration constamment à l'esprit, s'efforcent, par l'enseignement et l'éducation, de développer le respect de ces droits et libertés et d'en assurer, par des mesures progressives d'ordre national et international, la reconnaissance et l'application universelles et effectives, tant parmi les populations des États Membres eux-mêmes que parmi celles des territoires placés sous leur juridiction.

Article premier

Tous les êtres humains naissent libres et égaux en dignité et en droits. Ils sont doués de raison et de conscience et doivent agir les uns envers les autres dans un esprit de fraternité.

Article 2

Chacun peut se prévaloir de tous les droits et de toutes les libertés proclamés dans la présente Déclaration, sans distinction aucune, notamment de race, de couleur, de sexe, de langue, de religion, d'opinion politique ou de toute autre opinion, d'origine nationale ou sociale, de fortune, de naissance ou de toute autre situation.

De plus, il ne sera fait aucune distinction fondée sur le statut politique, juridique ou international du pays ou du territoire dont une personne est ressortissante, que ce pays ou territoire soit indépendant, sous tutelle, non autonome ou soumis à une limitation quelconque de souveraineté.

Article 3

Tout individu a droit à la vie, à la liberté et à la sûreté de sa personne.

Article 4

Nul ne sera tenu en esclavage ni en servitude ; l'esclavage et la traite des esclaves sont interdits sous toutes leurs formes.

— 3 —

Article 5

Nul ne sera soumis à la torture, ni à des peines ou traitements cruels, inhumains ou dégradants.

Article 6

Chacun a le droit à la reconnaissance en tous lieux de sa personnalité juridique.

Article 7

Tous sont égaux devant la loi et ont droit sans distinction à une égale protection de la loi. Tous ont droit à une protection égale contre toute discrimination qui violerait la présente Déclaration et contre toute provocation à une telle discrimination.

Article 8

Toute personne a droit à un recours effectif devant les juridictions nationales compétentes contre les actes violant les droits fondamentaux qui lui sont reconnus par la constitution ou par la loi.

Article 9

Nul ne peut être arbitrairement arrêté, détenu ou exilé.

Article 10

Toute personne a droit, en pleine égalité, à ce que sa cause soit entendue équitablement et publiquement par un tribunal indépendant et impartial, qui décidera, soit de ses droits et obligations, soit du bien-fondé de toute accusation en matière pénale dirigée contre elle.

Article 11

(1) Toute personne accusée d'un acte délictueux est présumée innocente jusqu'à ce que sa culpabilité ait été légalement établie au cours d'un procès public où toutes les garanties nécessaires à sa défense lui auront été assurées.

(2) Nul ne sera condamné pour des actions ou omissions qui, au moment où elles ont été commises, ne constituaient pas un acte délictueux d'après le droit national ou international. De même, il ne sera infligé aucune peine plus forte que celle qui était applicable au moment où l'acte délictueux a été commis.

— 4 —

Article 12

Nul ne sera l'objet d'immixtions arbitraires dans sa vie privée, sa famille, son domicile ou sa correspondance, ni d'atteintes à son honneur et à sa réputation. Toute personne a droit à la protection de la loi contre de telles immixtions ou de telles atteintes.

Article 13

(1) Toute personne a le droit de circuler librement et de choisir sa résidence à l'intérieur d'un État.

(2) Toute personne a le droit de quitter tout pays, y compris le sien, et de revenir dans son pays.

Article 14

(1) Devant la persécution, toute personne a le droit de chercher asile et de bénéficier de l'asile en d'autres pays.

(2) Ce droit ne peut être invoqué dans le cas de poursuites réellement fondées sur un crime de droit commun ou sur des agissements contraires aux buts et aux principes des Nations Unies.

Article 15

(1) Tout individu a droit à une nationalité.

(2) Nul ne peut être arbitrairement privé de sa nationalité, ni du droit de changer de nationalité.

Article 16

(1) A partir de l'âge nubile, l'homme et la femme, sans aucune restriction quant à la race, la nationalité ou la religion, ont le droit de se marier et de fonder une famille. Ils ont des droits égaux au regard du mariage, durant le mariage et lors de sa dissolution.

(2) Le mariage ne peut être conclu qu'avec le libre et plein consentement des futurs époux.

(3) La famille est l'élément naturel et fondamental de la société et a droit à la protection de la société et de l'État.

Article 17

(1) Toute personne, aussi bien seule qu'en collectivité, a droit à la propriété.

(2) Nul ne peut être arbitrairement privé de sa propriété.

— 5 —

tolérance et l'amitié entre toutes les nations et tous les groupes raciaux ou religieux, ainsi que le développement des activités des Nations Unies pour le maintien de la paix.

(3) Les parents ont, par priorité, le droit de choisir le genre d'éducation à donner à leurs enfants.

Article 27

(1) Toute personne a le droit de prendre part librement à la vie culturelle de la communauté, de jouir des arts et de participer au progrès scientifique et aux bienfaits qui en résultent.

(2) Chacun a droit à la protection des intérêts moraux et matériels découlant de toute production scientifique, littéraire ou artistique dont il est l'auteur.

Article 28

Toute personne a droit à ce que règne, sur le plan social et sur le plan international, un ordre tel que les droits et libertés énoncés dans la présente Déclaration puissent y trouver plein effet.

Article 29

(1) L'individu a des devoirs envers la communauté dans laquelle seule le libre et plein développement de sa personnalité est possible.

(2) Dans l'exercice de ses droits et dans la jouissance de ses libertés, chacun n'est soumis qu'aux limitations établies par la loi exclusivement en vue d'assurer la reconnaissance et le respect des droits et libertés d'autrui et afin de satisfaire aux justes exigences de la morale, de l'ordre public et du bien-être général dans une société démocratique.

(3) Ces droits et libertés ne pourront, en aucun cas, s'exercer contrairement aux buts et aux principes des Nations Unies.

Article 30

Aucune disposition de la présente Déclaration ne peut être interprétée comme impliquant pour un État, un groupement ou un individu un droit quelconque de se livrer à une activité ou d'accomplir un acte visant à la destruction des droits et libertés qui y sont énoncés.

Reprinted in U.N., N.Y.   OPI/15—09273-May 1972-100M

Article 18

Toute personne a droit à la liberté de pensée, de conscience et de religion ; ce droit implique la liberté de changer de religion ou de conviction ainsi que la liberté de manifester sa religion ou sa conviction seule ou en commun, tant en public qu'en privé, par l'enseignement, les pratiques, le culte et l'accomplissement des rites.

Article 19

Tout individu a droit à la liberté d'opinion et d'expression, ce qui implique le droit de ne pas être inquiété pour ses opinions et celui de chercher, de recevoir et de répandre, sans considérations de frontières, les informations et les idées par quelque moyen d'expression que ce soit.

Article 20

(1) Toute personne a droit à la liberté de réunion et d'association pacifiques.

(2) Nul ne peut être obligé de faire partie d'une association.

Article 21

(1) Toute personne a le droit de prendre part à la direction des affaires publiques de son pays, soit directement, soit par l'intermédiaire de représentants librement choisis.

(2) Toute personne a droit à accéder, dans des conditions d'égalité, aux fonctions publiques de son pays.

(3) La volonté du peuple est le fondement de l'autorité des pouvoirs publics ; cette volonté doit s'exprimer par des élections honnêtes qui doivent avoir lieu périodiquement, au suffrage universel égal et au vote secret ou suivant une procédure équivalente assurant la liberté du vote.

Article 22

Toute personne, en tant que membre de la société, a droit à la sécurité sociale ; elle est fondée à obtenir la satisfaction des droits économiques, sociaux et culturels indispensables à sa dignité et au libre développement de sa personnalité, grâce à l'effort national et à la coopération internationale, compte tenu de l'organisation et des ressources de chaque pays.

Article 23

(1) Toute personne a droit au travail, au libre choix de son travail, à des conditions équitables et satisfai-

— 6 —

DÉCLARATION UNIVERSELLE des DROITS DE L'HOMME

LE 10 DÉCEMBRE 1948, l'Assemblée générale des Nations Unies a adopté et proclamé la Déclaration universelle des droits de l'homme dont nous publions le texte. Après cet acte historique, l'Assemblée générale a recommandé aux Etats Membres de ne négliger aucun des moyens en leur pouvoir pour publier solennellement le texte de la Déclaration et « pour faire en sorte qu'il soit distribué, affiché, lu et commenté principalement dans les écoles et autres établissements d'enseignement, sans distinction fondée sur le statut politique des pays ou des territoires ».

SERVICE DE L'INFORMATION
DES NATIONS UNIES

Distribuée par:

WORLD SERVICE AUTHORITY
1012 14th Street, N.W. - Suite 1106
Washington, D.C. 20005 - USA

santes de travail et à la protection contre le chômage.

(2) Tous ont droit, sans aucune discrimination, à un salaire égal pour un travail égal.

(3) Quiconque travaille a droit à une rémunération équitable et satisfaisante lui assurant ainsi qu'à sa famille une existence conforme à la dignité humaine et complétée, s'il y a lieu, par tous autres moyens de protection sociale.

(4) Toute personne a le droit de fonder avec d'autres des syndicats et de s'affilier à des syndicats pour la défense de ses intérêts.

Article 24

Toute personne a droit au repos et aux loisirs et notamment à une limitation raisonnable de la durée du travail et à des congés payés périodiques.

Article 25

(1) Toute personne a droit à un niveau de vie suffisant pour assurer sa santé, son bien-être et ceux de sa famille, notamment pour l'alimentation, l'habillement, le logement, les soins médicaux ainsi que pour les services sociaux nécessaires ; elle a droit à la sécurité en cas de chômage, de maladie, d'invalidité, de veuvage, de vieillesse ou dans les autres cas de perte de ses moyens de subsistance par suite de circonstances indépendantes de sa volonté.

(2) La maternité et l'enfance ont droit à une aide et à une assistance spéciales. Tous les enfants, qu'ils soient nés dans le mariage ou hors mariage, jouissent de la même protection sociale.

Article 26

(1) Toute personne a droit à l'éducation. L'éducation doit être gratuite, au moins en ce qui concerne l'enseignement élémentaire et fondamental. L'enseignement élémentaire est obligatoire. L'enseignement technique et professionnel doit être généralisé ; l'accès aux études supérieures doit être ouvert en pleine égalité à tous en fonction de leur mérite.

(2) L'éducation doit viser au plein épanouissement de la personnalité humaine et au renforcement du respect des droits de l'homme et des libertés fondamentales. Elle doit favoriser la compréhension, la

— 7 —

DECLARACION UNIVERSAL DE DERECHOS HUMANOS

PREAMBULO

Considerando que la libertad, la justicia y la paz en el mundo tienen por base el reconocimiento de la dignidad intrínseca y de los derechos iguales e inalienables de todos los miembros de la familia humana;

Considerando que el desconocimiento y el menosprecio de los derechos humanos han originado actos de barbarie ultrajantes para la conciencia de la humanidad, y que se ha proclamado, como la aspiración más elevada del hombre, el advenimiento de un mundo en que los seres humanos, liberados del temor y de la miseria, disfruten de la libertad de palabra y de la libertad de creencias;

Considerando esencial que los derechos humanos sean protegidos por un régimen de Derecho, a fin de que el hombre no se vea compelido al supremo recurso de la rebelión contra la tiranía y la opresión;

Considerando también esencial promover el desarrollo de relaciones amistosas entre las naciones;

Considerando que los pueblos de las Naciones Unidas han reafirmado en la Carta, su fe en los derechos fundamentales del hombre, en la dignidad y el valor de la persona humana y en la igualdad de derechos de hombres y mujeres; y se han declarado resueltos a promover el progreso social y a elevar el nivel de vida dentro de un concepto más amplio de la libertad;

Considerando que los Estados Miembros se han comprometido a asegurar, en cooperación con la Organización de las Naciones Unidas, el respeto universal y efectivo a los derechos y libertades fundamentales del hombre; y

Considerando que una concepción común de estos derechos y libertades es de la mayor importancia para el pleno cumplimiento de dicho compromiso;

2

LA ASAMBLEA GENERAL

proclama la presente

DECLARACION UNIVERSAL DE DERECHOS HUMANOS

como ideal común por el que todos los pueblos y naciones deben esforzarse, a fin de que tanto los individuos como las instituciones, inspirándose constantemente en ella, promuevan, mediante la enseñanza y la educación, el respeto a estos derechos y libertades, y aseguren, por medidas progresivas de carácter nacional e internacional, su reconocimiento y aplicación universales y efectivos, tanto entre los pueblos de los Estados Miembros como entre los de los territorios colocados bajo su jurisdicción.

Artículo 1

Todos los seres humanos nacen libres e iguales en dignidad y derechos y, dotados como están de razón y conciencia, deben comportarse fraternalmente los unos con los otros.

Artículo 2

1. Toda persona tiene todos los derechos y libertades proclamados en esta Declaración, sin distinción alguna de raza, color, sexo, idioma, religión, opinión política o de cualquier otra índole, origen nacional o social, posición económica, nacimiento o cualquier otra condición.

2. Además, no se hará distinción alguna fundada en la condición política, jurídica o internacional del país o territorio de cuya jurisdicción dependa una persona, tanto si se trata de un país independiente, como de un territorio bajo administración fiduciaria, no autónomo o sometido a cualquier otra limitación de soberanía.

Artículo 3

Todo individuo tiene derecho a la vida, a la libertad y a la seguridad de su persona.

Artículo 4

Nadie estará sometido a esclavitud ni a servidumbre, la esclavitud y la trata de esclavos están prohibidas en todas sus formas.

3

Artículo 5

Nadie será sometido a torturas ni a penas o tratos crueles, inhumanos o degradantes.

Artículo 6

Todo ser humano tiene derecho, en todas partes, al reconocimiento de su personalidad jurídica.

Artículo 7

Todos son iguales ante la ley y tienen, sin distinción, derecho a igual protección de la ley. Todos tienen derecho a igual protección contra toda discriminación que infrinja esta Declaración y contra toda provocación a tal discriminación.

Artículo 8

Toda persona tiene derecho a un recurso efectivo, ante los tribunales nacionales competentes, que la ampare contra actos que violen sus derechos fundamentales reconocidos por la constitución o por la ley.

Artículo 9

Nadie podrá ser arbitrariamente detenido, preso ni desterrado.

Artículo 10

Toda persona tiene derecho, en condiciones de plena igualdad, a ser oída públicamente y con justicia por un tribunal independiente e imparcial, para la determinación de sus derechos y obligaciones o para el examen de cualquier acusación contra ella en materia penal.

Artículo 11

1. Toda persona acusada de delito tiene derecho a que se presuma su inocencia mientras no se pruebe su culpabilidad, conforme a la ley y en juicio público en el que se le hayan asegurado todas las garantías necesarias para su defensa.

2. Nadie será condenado por actos u omisiones que en el momento de cometerse no fueron delictivos según el Derecho nacional o internacional. Tampoco se impondrá pena más grave que la aplicable en el momento de la comisión del delito.

4

Artículo 12

Nadie será objeto de ingerencias arbitrarias en su vida privada, su familia, su domicilio o su correspondencia, ni de ataques a su honra o a su reputación. Toda persona tiene derecho a la protección de la ley contra tales ingerencias o ataques.

Artículo 13

1. Toda persona tiene derecho a circular libremente y a elegir su residencia en el territorio de un Estado.

2. Toda persona tiene derecho a salir de cualquier país, incluso del propio, y a regresar a su país.

Artículo 14

1. En caso de persecución, toda persona tiene derecho a buscar asilo, y a disfrutar de él, en cualquier país.

2. Este derecho no podrá ser invocado contra una acción judicial realmente originada por delitos comunes o por actos opuestos a los propósitos y principios de las Naciones Unidas.

Artículo 15

1. Toda persona tiene derecho a una nacionalidad.

2. A nadie se privará arbitrariamente de su nacionalidad ni del derecho a cambiar de nacionalidad.

Artículo 16

1. Los hombres y las mujeres, a partir de la edad núbil, tienen derecho, sin restricción alguna por motivos de raza, nacionalidad o religión, a casarse y fundar una familia; y disfrutarán de iguales derechos en cuanto al matrimonio, durante el matrimonio y en caso de disolución del matrimonio.

2. Sólo mediante libre y pleno consentimiento de los futuros esposos podrá contraerse el matrimonio.

3. La familia es el elemento natural y fundamental de la sociedad y tiene derecho a la protección de la sociedad y del Estado.

Artículo 17

1. Toda persona tiene derecho a la propiedad, individual y colectivamente.

2. Nadie será privado arbitrariamente de su propiedad.

5

amistad entre todas las naciones y todos los grupos étnicos o religiosos; y promoverá el desarrollo de las actividades de las Naciones Unidas para el mantenimiento de la paz.

3. Los padres tendrán derecho preferente a escoger el tipo de educación que habrá de darse a sus hijos.

Artículo 27

1. Toda persona tiene derecho a tomar parte libremente en la vida cultural de la comunidad, a gozar de las artes y a participar en el progreso científico y en los beneficios que de él resulten.

2. Toda persona tiene derecho a la protección de los intereses morales y materiales que le correspondan por razón de las producciones científicas, literarias o artísticas de que sea autora.

Artículo 28

Toda persona tiene derecho a que se establezca un orden social e internacional en el que los derechos y libertades proclamados en esta Declaración se hagan plenamente efectivos.

Artículo 29

1. Toda persona tiene deberes respecto a la comunidad, puesto que sólo en ella puede desarrollar libre y plenamente su personalidad.

2. En el ejercicio de sus derechos y en el disfrute de sus libertades, toda persona estará solamente sujeta a las limitaciones establecidas por la ley con el único fin de asegurar el reconocimiento y el respeto de los derechos y libertades de los demás, y de satisfacer las justas exigencias de la moral, del orden público y del bienestar general en una sociedad democrática.

3. Estos derechos y libertades no podrán, en ningún caso, ser ejercidos en oposición a los propósitos y principios de las Naciones Unidas.

Artículo 30

Nada en esta Declaración podrá interpretarse en el sentido de que confiere derecho alguno al Estado, a un grupo o a una persona, para emprender y desarrollar actividades o realizar actos tendientes a la supresión de cualquiera de los derechos y libertades proclamados en esta Declaración.

Universal Declaration of Human Rights (Spanish)

Reprinted in U.N. DPI/15—22835—September 1988—50M

Artículo 18

Toda persona tiene derecho a la libertad de pensamiento, de conciencia y de religión; este derecho incluye la libertad de cambiar de religión o de creencia, así como la libertad de manifestar su religión o su creencia, individual y colectivamente, tanto en público como en privado, por la enseñanza, la práctica, el culto y la observancia.

Artículo 19

Todo individuo tiene derecho a la libertad de opinión y de expresión; este derecho incluye el de no ser molestado a causa de sus opiniones, el de investigar y recibir informaciones y opiniones, y el de difundirlas, sin limitación de fronteras, por cualquier medio de expresión.

Artículo 20

1. Toda persona tiene derecho a la libertad de reunión y de asociación pacíficas.

2. Nadie podrá ser obligado a pertenecer a una asociación.

Artículo 21

1. Toda persona tiene derecho a participar en el gobierno de su país, directamente o por medio de representantes libremente escogidos.

2. Toda persona tiene el derecho de acceso, en condiciones de igualdad, a las funciones públicas de su país.

3. La voluntad del pueblo es la base de la autoridad del poder público; esta voluntad se expresará mediante elecciones auténticas que habrán de celebrarse periódicamente, por sufragio universal e igual y por voto secreto u otro procedimiento equivalente que garantice la libertad del voto.

Artículo 22

Toda persona, como miembro de la sociedad, tiene derecho a la seguridad social, y a obtener, mediante el esfuerzo nacional y la cooperación internacional, habida cuenta de la organización y los recursos de cada Estado, la satisfacción de los derechos económicos, sociales y culturales, indispensables a su dignidad y al libre desarrollo de su personalidad.

DECLARACION
UNIVERSAL
de
DERECHOS HUMANOS

Aprobada y proclamada por la Asamblea General de las Naciones Unidas el 10 de diciembre de 1948

El 10 DE DICIEMBRE DE 1948 la Asamblea General de las Naciones Unidas aprobó y proclamó la Declaración Universal de Derechos Humanos, cuyo texto completo aparece en las siguientes páginas. A continuación de ese acto histórico, recomendó la Asamblea a todos los Estados Miembros que publicaran el texto de la Declaración y procuraran que fuese "divulgado, expuesta, leída y comentada, principalmente en las escuelas y demás establecimientos de enseñanza, sin distinción alguna, basada en la situación política de los países o de los territorios."

DEPARTAMENTO DE INFORMACION PUBLICA DE LAS NACIONES UNIDAS
Distribuido por:
WORLD SERVICE AUTHORITY
1012 14th Street, N.W. - Suite 1106
Washington, D.C. 20005 - USA
tele: (202)638-2662 Fax: (202)638-0638

Artículo 23

1. Toda persona tiene derecho al trabajo, a la libre elección de su trabajo, a condiciones equitativas y satisfactorias de trabajo y a la protección contra el desempleo.

2. Toda persona tiene derecho, sin discriminación alguna, a igual salario por trabajo igual.

3. Toda persona que trabaja tiene derecho a una remuneración equitativa y satisfactoria, que le asegure, así como a su familia, una existencia conforme a la dignidad humana y que será completada, en caso necesario, por cualesquiera otros medios de protección social.

4. Toda persona tiene derecho a fundar sindicatos y a sindicarse para la defensa de sus intereses.

Artículo 24

Toda persona tiene derecho al descanso, al disfrute del tiempo libre, a una limitación razonable de la duración del trabajo y a vacaciones periódicas pagadas.

Artículo 25

1. Toda persona tiene derecho a un nivel de vida adecuado que le asegure, así como a su familia, la salud y el bienestar, y en especial la alimentación, el vestido, la vivienda, la asistencia médica y los servicios sociales necesarios; tiene asimismo derecho a los seguros en caso de desempleo, enfermedad, invalidez, viudez, vejez u otros casos de pérdida de sus medios de subsistencia por circunstancias independientes de su voluntad.

2. La maternidad y la infancia tienen derecho a cuidados y asistencia especiales. Todos los niños, nacidos de matrimonio o fuera de matrimonio, tienen derecho a igual protección social.

Artículo 26

1. Toda persona tiene derecho a la educación. La educación debe ser gratuita, al menos en lo concerniente a la instrucción elemental y fundamental. La instrucción elemental será obligatoria. La instrucción técnica y profesional habrá de ser generalizada; el acceso a los estudios superiores será igual para todos, en función de los méritos respectivos.

2. La educación tendrá por objeto el pleno desarrollo de la personalidad humana y el fortalecimiento del respeto a los derechos humanos y a las libertades fundamentales; favorecerá la comprensión, la tolerancia y la

Index

Accounting, 151
Acheson, Dean, 19
Africa, 56, 60, 167, 168
Akihito, Emperor, 169
Albania, 60
Algeria, 8
Alien, 7
Alienation, 148
Allenby Bridge, 90
Alternative national service, 133
Anatomy of Peace, 121, 157
Aptheker v. Secretary of State, 63
Arabs, 47
Armenians, 54
Arms race, 7, 25, 157, 167
Asia, 139, 168, 170
Asia Magazine, 170
Asimov, Isaac, 1, 175
Assignment editors, 160, 162
Associated Press, 112
Asylum, 78–79
    political, 138

Baha'u'llah, 3
Ball-Wilson, Harry, 175
Baltic states, 169
Bangladesh, 167
BankAmerica, 152
Beer, Stafford, 158–159, 175
Belgium, 143
Berlin, 7
Berlin Conference, 56
Berlin wall, 143
Berne, 160
Big government, 147
Biosphere. 158
Birth, 12, 131
Birth certificate, 131
Blackstone, Justice Willian, 37
Bombay, 40
Bonn, 125
Bordeaux, 142

Borders, 28–29
Boston, 142
Boyle, Francis, 175
Brandt, Willy, 33–34
Brazil, 18
British Honduras, 35
Brixton prison, 124
Bulgaria, 89, 169
Bureaucracy, 26, 30–31, 33, 36, 45
Bureaucrats, 16–17, 26
Burkina Faso (Upper Volta), 67, 93
Bush, President George, 136, 166,
    167, 168

Cahors, 140
Cameroon, 35
Canada, 54
    mundialization in, 142
Capital, 147–148,
    workers and, 150, 153
    money and, 151
Capital investment, 147
Carter, President James, 119, 167
Cassid, Syd, 175
Center for Economic and Social
    Justice, 146
Central Banks, 152
Central Europe, 167
Chaggara, 137–138
Champaign, ILL, 83
Chapman, Christine, 102
Charter of Solidarity, 141
China, 167, 169
Chinese expatriates, 78
Churchill, Winston, 119
Citizen, 32
    international economic, 153
    mundialization and, 142
Civic ownership, 153
Civil Disobedience, 135
Clarke, Arthur, 1
Cold War, 8, 63, 121, 167

Collective will, 12
Cologne, 169
Commonweal, 156
Communist bloc, 11
Community, 19
Complexity, management of, 159
Conscientious objection, 133, 134
Conscription, 130
    alternative to, 133
    refusal of, 131
    world citizenship and, 132
Constitution, U.S., 20, 63
    Ninth Amendment to, 91, 135
Constructive notice, 74
Consumers, 152
Cook Islands, 60
Corporations, 145–146
    capital investment and, 147
    money and, 151
Covenant of peace, 120
Crime, 148
Currency, 145, 151, 154
Cybernetics, 158, 159
Cyprus, 89, 169
Czechoslovakia, 89, 139, 169

Dalai Lama, 95
Danzig, Free City of, 138
Davis, Garry, 1–3, 175
    in Brixton Prison, 125
    court cases of, 91–92
    returns to Europe, 169
    as excludable alien, 91, 114, 170
    as first world citizen, 22
    France prosecutes, 67, 89
    French visa issued to, 22
    in Holland, 42
    visits India, 39
    INS and, 107–114
    on international territory,
        139–140
    in Iran, 40
    in Israel, 89
    visits Japan, 93–105
    Japan deports, 170
    establishes Japanese office,
        168–169
    holds press conference, 160
    enters U.S., 32, 43–44, 90, 115

    renounces U.S. citizenship, 14
    World Passport of, 89
    in World War II, 7
Declaration of Independence, 138
Degrees, 16
Democracy, 46
    economic, 152–153
    ownership and, 147–150
    political representation in a, 138
Democratic ownership, 149–150
Deportation, 34, 35, 91, 170
Diplomats, 81
Disarmament, 7
Documents, 16, 27
Domination, 144
    of nature, 2
Douglas, William O., 91
Dow, Mr., 109, 111–112
Drugs, 53
Dundas, 142
Dunham, Katherine, 175
Du Val-De-Grace, Jean Baptiste, 120
Dynamic Identification, four levels
    of, 24–25
    fourth level of, 158

East Berlin, 169
Eastern Europe, 166, 169
Ecological crisis, 2, 167
Economic justice, 154
Economic opportunity, 48
Economic rights, 152–154
Economics, 145
    big government and, 147
    distributive, 149
    scarcity model of, 151
    SDRs and, 153
    World Government, 150
Ecuador, 67, 93
Egypt, 35
Einstein, Albert, 8, 9, 56, 119
Eisenhower, President Dwight, 63,
    133
Elections, 12
Ellsworth, ME, 126
    world territory declared in, 141
Employee Stock Ownership Plans
    (ESOPs), 153, 154
Equal pay, 154

Esperanto, 66, 68, 70
Ethnic rivalries, 54, 167
European economic community, 53
Exchange value, 150
Excludable alien, 91, 114, 170
Expatriation Act, 17

Fascism, 7
Federation, 9
Feudalism, 56
Filartiga v. Pena-Irala, 162
Flight Terminal Security Co., 105
Ford, President Gerald, 167
Forest Hills, NY, 133
France, 11, 14, 22, 67, 120, 125, 128,
    138, 140
  introduces passports, 61
  Middle East boundaries and, 56
French-Swiss border, 137
Frontier guards, 81
Frontiers, 28
Full employment, 147
Fuller, Buckminster, 151, 159

Gandhi, 9, 135
  uniforms and, 160
General affluence, 147
General Motors, 145
Geneva, 2
Geodesic dome, 159
Geosphere, 158
Germany, 7, 10
  Commissioner of Foreign Police,
    33
  Garry Davis in, 42, 169
  marriage in, 77
  mundialization in, 140, 143
  sovereignty in, 18
  World Citizens in, 125
  World Passport and, 33–34, 35–36
Ghana, 35
Ginza, 102
Global economic order, 155
Global Mutual Fund, 150
Global rights, 128
Global village, 24, 47, 54, 144
Gorbachev, Mikhail, 135
Gold, 151
Goldsmith, Edward, 175

Great Britain, 11
  Middle East boundaries and, 56,
    136
  nationalism and, 46
  passport system in, 61
Greece, 18
Gross national product, 145
Guilt, 84
Gulf War, 136, 166

Haas, Fred, 133–135
Hague Treaty, 120
Haiti, 89
Hamburg, 35
Havel, Vaclav, 169
Hayes, Arthur Garfield, 125
Hesei, 169
Hesingue, 137
Higher Law, 133
Hirohito, Emperor, 93, 95
Hirosaki University, 96
Hiroshima, 95, 142
Holism, 25, 123, 137, 144, 158
Holland, 42–43
Holy See, 137–138
Homstead Act, 17
Hong Kong, 60, 78, 170
Hopkins, Mr., 113–114
Humanity, 12, 13, 24, 171
  brain of, 48
  as higher authority, 122
  lover of, 48
  sovereignty of, 20–21, 156–157
  spiritual needs of, 148
  unity of, 164
  world constitution and, 158
Human Rights, 11, 29, 34, 37–38,
    53, 57, 94, 120, 122, 127, 138,
    168
  asylum and, 78
  conscription and, 131
  economic, 154
  elections and, 162
  enumerated, 82–83
  national law and, 73
  national security and, 19
  sovereignty and, 25
  UN Commission on, 128
Hyatt Regency, 112

Illinois, 142
Immigrants, 17
Immigration and Nationality Act, 63, 111
Immigration and Naturalization Service (INS), 90, 107–108, 111–114, 170
Immigration jail, 110, 170
Imperialism, 146, 167
Inalienable rights, 20, 25, 59, 91, 113
Income, 146, 147
India, 1, 3, 11, 40, 42, 89, 133, 135, 143
    mundialization in, 143
Indonesia, 170
Infosets, 158–159
Interdependence, 144
International Court of Justice, 20, 128
International Covenant on Civil and Political Rights, 35, 86
International Covenant on Human Rights, 72
International Exit Visa, 79
International Herald Tribune, 102
International Institute for Strategic Studies, 57
International law, 19–20, 72, 87, 128, 132, 134, 138
    asylum and, 79
    conscription and, 130–131
    crime and, 130
    territory and, 137
International Law Commission of Jurists, 19
International Monetary Fund, 152
International Refugee Organization, 62
International Registry of World Citizens, 23, 125
International Resident Permit, 79–80
International territory, 137–138
    Palais de Chaillot as, 140
Iowa, 142
Iran, 40, 42
Iraq, 136
Israel, 8, 89–90, 136
    founding of, 139
    marriage in, 77
    military service in, 133

Italy, 137–138
    mundialization in, 143

Japan, 68, 78, 94–105, 169, 170
    constitution of, 18, 96
    Golden Week, 96
    Immigration Service, 170
    Ministry of Justice, 103
    mundialization in, 141, 143
    New World Order and, 167
Japan Congress Against A and H-Bombs, 96
Japanese Immigration Service, 170
Japan Times, 95, 102
Jerusalem, 89, 143
Jesus Christ, 3
Jones, Judge Newton, 113–114
Jordan, 8, 90
Jus Sanguinis, 131
Jus Solis, 131

Kaga, 142
Kaifu, Toshiki, 170
Kaplan v. Todd, 114
Kant, Immanuel, 120
Kashmir, 8
Kaya, Yusuf, 33–34, 35, 41
    marriage of, 77–78
Kennedy Airport, 90
Kenya, 8
Kissinger, Henry, 167
KLM, 42
Korea, 8
Korean War, 63
Kurds, 54, 167
Kurland, Norman, 146
Kushi, Michio, 175
Kutner, Dr. Luis, 128
Kuwait, 136–137, 167

Ladewig, Jurgen, 175
Landsbergis, Vytautis, 169–170
Lateran Treaty, 137
League of Nations, 62, 120, 138, 167
Leisure, 154
Lenz, Badi, 175
Letter writing, 36–37, 39
Lifeboat ethics, 80

Ling, Mr., 99
Lithuania, 169
Lloyd, Georgia, 175
Los Angeles, CA, 24, 170
    mundialized, 141
London, 24, 90
Love, 1
Lovelock, James, 175
Luxembourg, 23

MacDonald, James Ramsey, 61
Mandela, Nelson, 135
Magna Carta, 13
Malaya, 8
Malaysia, 170
Manu's Laws, 13
Marriage, 77
Mass communication, 46
    use of, 160–162
Mauritania, 67, 93
McLuhan, Marshall, 47
Menuhin, Sir Yehudi, 175
Mexico, 89, 169
Mexico City, 24
Meyer, Cord, 9
Middle East, 48, 56, 89, 139
Military spending, 80, 141, 157
    elimination of, 148
    tax refusal and, 163
Minneapolis, MN, 142
Minnesota, mundial declaration of,
    142
Monetary distrust, 151
Money, 150–151
Money Market Funds, 150
Moscow, 170
Multinationals, 145, 148, 149, 151
    labor and, 153–154
    liquidity and, 152
    shares in, 153
Mundialization, 140–143, 162, 170
    activities, 143
    basic provisions of, 141
    charter, 140
    defined, 140–141
    movement grows, 142–143
Mutual Affluence System, 150
Mutual funds, 153

Nader, Ralph, 145, 147
Nagasaki, 95
    mundialized, 142
Name recognition, 161
Nansen, Fridtjof, 62
Nansen Office of Refugees, 62
Nansen passport, 62
Narita Airport, 94, 170
Narita Rest House, 96
Nataraji Guru, 1–3, 135
Nation, 54, 122
National currencies, 151
National citizenship, 7, 38, 57, 73, 121
    birth and, 131
    ownership and, 149
    world order and, 167–168
Nationalism, 38, 127, 167
    growth of, 46–47
    mundialization and, 143
National security, 19, 57, 133, 136
Nation-state, 2, 14–15, 25, 46–47, 127,
        133, 144, 149, 156, 157, 159,
        168, 170, 171
    birthright and, 131
    characteristics of, 56–57
    concept of, 54
    conscientious objection status in,
        133
    economics, 145, 148
    erosion of, 53–54
    humanity and, 122
    marriage and, 77
    money and, 151
    passports and, 61
    population and, 24
    territory and, 136
    trust and, 150
    war and, 9, 120
NATO, 54, 64
Natural rights, 20, 37, 45–46, 92, 122
Nehru, 43
Newcombe, Hanna, 142
New World Order, 166–168
New York, NY, 24, 40
New Zealand, 89
Nicholas, Czar, 120
Nimes, 142
Nixon, President Richard, 167
Nobel Laureates' Forum, 170

Nobel Peace Prize, 62
Noel, Henry, 10
Non-Governmental Organizations (NGOs), 64
Nonviolence, 88
Northwest Orient, 93, 96, 100, 105
Norway, 62
Nuclear weapons, 7–8, 57, 120, 141
Nuremberg Principles, 13, 19–20, 129, 130
    international rights under, 138
    pentagon and, 134
    taxes and, 162
Nyerere, Julius, 119
Nysox, Mr., 107, 108

Oath of Renunciation, 14
Oil, 136
Omnicide, 7
One World, 9
Ontario, 142
Ootacamond, 1
Organized labor. See unions
Ottoman empire, 54, 56
Ottawa, 142
Ownership, 24, 144, 151
    concentration of, 148
    democratic, 146, 149
    multinationals and, 148

Pacific rim, 168, 170
Pacifism, 133
Paine, Thomas, 122
Pakistan, 42
Palais de Chaillot, 140
Palestinians, 54, 136
Paquette v. Habana, 163
Paris, 139–140
Passports, 14, 59–65
    authority to issue, 63
    civil servants and, 64
    history of, 61–62
    revoking of, 60
    sailors and, 64
    visas for, 60
    uses of, 63
Peace or Anarchy, 9
Peace organizations, 157
Pentagon, 134, 135

Perk, William, 175
Permanent Court of International Justice, 138
Peru, 89, 169
Pirates, 47
Planetary dictatorship, 168
Planning, 48
Pledge of Allegiance, World, 165
Political prisoners, 128
Police, 132
Pollution, 53, 157, 167
Pont Kehl, 125
Popov, Gavril, 170
Poverty, 150, 151
Press, 87, 112, 160
    Freedom of, 161
Press releases, 160, 161–162
Profits, 149–150, 151
Property, 146–147, 154
Protective custody, 60
Protectorates, 138
Purchasing power, 147, 153

Quakers, 78

Reagan, President Ronald, 16, 93, 167
Red Cross, 64
Refugees, 26, 69, 80, 157
    asylum and, 78, 123
    passports and, 61–62
    WSA assistance to, 127, 128–129, 163
Religion, 3
Remuneration, 154
Renan, Ernest, 61
Renton City Jail, 113
Reserve Asset, 151
Reves, Emery, 121, 156
Richfield, OH, 142
Riggs National Bank, 152
Rights, 37–38
Romania, 89, 169
Roppangi, 102
Rosin, Carol S., 175
Russell, Bertrand, 9

Saddam Hussein, 136
Safire, William, 167
Saint Louis, 141

Sakharov, Andrei, 170
Salvadorans, 78
San Francisco, CA, 96, 99
Sannyasin, 2, 135
Satellite conferencing, 158
Saudi Arabia, 42
Schmidt, Helmut, 35
Schweitzer, Albert, 9
Seattle, WA, 105, 106
Security, 11, 13, 25
Self-determination, 35, 54, 87, 138,
    168
Selective service, 133
    fear of publicty, 134
    human rights and, 134
Singapore, 89, 170
Sister cities, 142, 143
Slavery, 137
Smith, Adam, 152
Social contract, 19, 23, 71, 80
Socrates, 161
Soldiers, 130–131, 132
South Africa, 35, 60
South Korea, 139
Sovereign Order of World Guards,
    39, 132–133, 134, 135
Sovereignty, 9–10, 17, 46, 48, 156, 160
    defined, 18
    of consumer, 145
    of humanity, 24
    national, 46, 53
    World Government and, 122
    World Passport and, 80
Soviet Union, 47, 139,
    decline of, 149, 169
    New World Order and, 167
Special Drawing Rights (SDRs),
    151–152
Sri Lanka, 54
Starvation, 157, 167
State, 54
Stockholm Declaration, 74, 129
Strasbourg, 90, 125
Sturgeon, Ted, 1
Suzuki, Shunichi, 170
Sweden, 18
Switzerland, 54, 60, 67, 90
    passport, 64

Taiwan, 170
Tanzania, 119
Tax refusal, 132, 162–163
Team tensegrity, 159
Technological revolution, 48, 54
Technosphere, 158
Telegraph, 46
Territoire Mondiale, 137
Territory, 47, 136
    holistic view of, 137
Terrorism, 53, 157
Thailand, 170
Thoreau, Henry, 135
Times of India, 40, 66
Toffler, Alvan, 53
Togo, 93
Tokyo, 24, 93, 94, 158, 169, 170
    mundialized, 142
Toronto, 158
    mundialized, 142
Transatlantic cable, 46
Travel, 63
Traveler's checks, 152
Treaty of Versailles, 138
Trieste, 8
Trieste, Free Territory of, 138
Trovilla, 140
Trust, 150
Truman, President Harry, 63
Tunisia, 35
Turkey, 33, 34
Twinning, 142, 143

Ultimatums, 40–41
Uniforms, 39–40, 133, 160
Unions, 148, 150, 153–154
United Europe, 155
United Nations, 2, 7, 20, 24, 32, 53,
    79, 120–121, 123, 137, 143, 167
    Articles 56 and 56, 83
    Charter of, 64, 67, 83, 95, 138
    Commission on Human Rights,
        128
    flag, 142
    General Assembly meets, 139
    High Commission for Refugees, 62
    international law and, 19
    refugees and, 62
    report on multinationals, 146

United Nations (*Continued*)
  Resolution 2625, 87
  Secretary General of, 64, 133, 142
  self-determination affirmed by, 138
  UNESCO, 64
  Universal Declaration of Human
    Rights adopted, 11
  war and, 8
United States, 8, 9–10, 47, 54, 61, 68,
  167
  Attorney General, 14
  Constitution of, 20, 73, 91, 135
  Department of Justice, 92, 114
  Department of State, 32, 63, 170
  dollar, 151
  economics in, 145
  Gulf War and, 166–167
  immigration to, 17, 78, 80
  mundialization and, 142
  nuclear weapons and, 57
  passport law adopted, 61
  Secretary of State, 63
  Supreme Court, 63, 92
  UN located in, 139
  visas required by, 60
United World Citizens Identity
  Card, 23
United World Federalists, 9
Universal Declaration of Human
  Rights, 11–13, 14, 33, 35, 67, 79,
  82, 86, 162
  Adoption of, 11
  Article 1, 11, 130–131
  Article 4, 130
  Article 13(1), 79
  Article 13(2), 29, 59, 75, 82, 90, 94
  Article 14, 79, 138
  Article 15(2), 72, 82, 138
  Article 16, 77
  Article 17, 146, 154
  Article 20, 154
  Article 21(3), 12, 13, 72, 138
  Article 23, 154
  Article 24, 154
  Article 25, 146
  Article 28, 12, 82
  Article 30, 83, 132
  asylum and, 78
  freedom to travel affirmed in, 32

  political allegiance and, 72–73
  soverignty affirmed in, 71
  World Government and, 122, 127

Vatican, city of, 138
Vietnam, 137
Vilnius, 169
Visas, 60, 79, 84, 169
von Teslon-Dennison, Ingrid, 175

Waldheim, Kurt, 33, 36
War, 7, 8, 9, 24, 577, 119–121, 130,
  141, 155, 156
  Nuremberg Principles and, 20
Washington, D.C., 90, 127, 128, 158
Washington Post, 53
WDR, 169
Wealth, 151
Webster, Daniel, 147
Wells, E.R., 175
Western Europe, 167
White, E.B., 123
Wiley, John, 112
Wilkie, Wendell, 9
Wilson, President Woodrow, 167
Wire services, 160
Wisconsin, 142
World Bank, 154
World Birth Certificate, 131–132
World Citizen Card, 74
World Citizens, 23, 67–68, 123, 126,
  140
  astronauts as, 65
  asylum and, 78–79
  conscription and, 133
  Credo of, 70
  defense of, 128
  experiences of, 89
  General Assembly of, 128
  Pledge of Allegiance, 165
  registering as, 74
  rights of, 67
  tax refusal and, 163
  union of, 153
  U.S. citizens as, 92
  World Constitution and,
    158–159
World Citizens for Constitutional
  Law, 157–159

World Citizenship, 23, 26, 44, 65, 120, 142, 156–157, 159, 169
  conscription and, 134
  early support for, 140
  French response to, 89
  holism and, 25
  national citizenship versus, 73
  nationalism and, 48–49
  necessity of, 72
  nonviolence and, 88
  ownership and, 149–150
  questions concerning, 72–76
  rationale for, 71
World Citizens Investors Corp., 153, 154
World Citizens Legal Fund, 128
World Citizens party, 74, 128, 162
World Citizens Point, 141
World City, 142
World Constitution, 158
  development process, 159
World Constitutional Convention, 158
World Court, 20
World Court of Human Rights, 36, 74, 86, 128
World federation, 9
World Flag, 143
World Government, 9, 23, 26, 33, 35, 74, 91, 92, 122, 125, 157
  attempts to create, 120
  constitution for, 158
  mundialization, 143
  ownership and, 149
  self-determination and, 87
  support for, 119
  territory and, 139
  Universal Declaration affirms, 13
  U.S. Citizens and, 134
World Government of World Citizens, 39, 87, 94, 143
  addresses, 163–164
  Annual Return Form, 163
  banking system, 129
  constitution for, 74
  declared, 137
  defined, 127
  description of, 74, 122–124
  documents of, 74
  finances of, 128–129

  founding of, 74, 126, 143
  marriage and, 78
  officers, 175
  operations, 128–129
  study commissions, 128
  territorial base declared, 137
  Treasury Department, 97, 163
World Government Treasury Account, 152
World Guards. See Sovereign Order of World Guards
World Judicial Commission, 83, 84, 86, 128
World law, 8, 20, 25, 34, 132, 141, 156, 158, 159, 169
World Marriage Certificate, 77–78
World Money, 96–97, 129, 150–152
World Mutual Abundance Bank, 163
World Organization of General Systems and Cybernetics, 158
World Passport, 28, 44, 40, 66–69, 123, 129, 160, 170
  case studies, 33–34, 35
  de facto recognition, 66
  de jure recognition, 67, 84
  countries recognizing, 66–67, 68, 75, 127
  gaining acceptance of, 81–84
  presented to world leaders, 169
  Sample visa booklet, 84
  transcending rejection of, 84–88
World peace, 24, 62, 158, 159,
World Police, 39, 134
World Political Asylum Card, 78
World Refugee Fund, 128, 129
World Registration Card, 33
World republic, 120
World Service Authority, 28, 33, 35, 123, 163, 169
  intervention by, 87–88
  issues documents, 67, 79
  law enforcement and, 76
  original intentions of, 126–127
  registration service, 74
  reporting to, 88
  significance of name, 39
  Tokyo office, 127, 170
  Washington, D.C. office, 90, 127, 170

World Territory, 89, 126, 137–139,
     140–141, 144, 162
World town, 140, 141
World trade, 154
World War I, 120
World War II, 7, 62, 120, 141, 166

Yati, Guru Nitya C., 175
Yemen, 93
Yomieri Shimbum, 95, 102

Zambia, 67, 93
Zimbabwe, 60